REGRETS OF A FOOTBALL MAVERICK
The Terry Curran Autobiography

REGRETS OF A FOOTBALL MAVERICK
The Terry Curran Autobiography

Terry Curran with John Brindley

Vertical Editions
www.verticaleditions.com

First published in the United Kingdom in 2012 by Vertical Editions,
Unit 4a, Snaygill Industrial Estate, Skipton, North Yorkshire BD23 2QR

www.verticaleditions.com

ISBN 978-1-904091-69-1

A CIP catalogue record for this book is available from the British Library

Cover design by HBA, York

Printed and bound by MPG, Bodmin

This book is dedicated with all my love to my sons Tom and Jock.

Terry Curran

Contents

Foreword

IT DOESN'T surprise me TC was voted Wednesday's all-time cult hero.

The fans loved him whilst I was at Hillsborough; he was a crowd pleaser. As a winger, he would take the ball up to the full back, drop his shoulder and he'd be gone. But, for me, he was even better as a central striker when we played him alongside his mate Andy McCulloch and he used some of the tricks he learned as a winger to beat his marker.

I enjoyed being at Hillsborough during largely good times for a famous club. We won promotion back to the Second Division in the season we beat Sheffield United 4-0 in the so-called Boxing Day Massacre. We then came close to getting into the old First Division before I left a good side and Howard Wilkinson took them up.

One reason for that success was I managed to nick Terry off my old friend Lawrie McMenemy at Southampton and persuaded him to drop down a couple of divisions to play for us. We got on well for most of the time but TC was funny – and I don't mean comical. He could do sensible things on the pitch, but could also be stupid. I never knew what the guy was going to do next. I remember backing him up to a wall in the gymnasium at Hillsborough although I've forgotten what the argument was about. Then there was that crazy moment against Derby County when he took the ball around the goalkeeper, sunk to his knees and headed the ball in. I got out of the box, ran up the touchline and wanted to kick the bugger's head off. He was a showman, TC, and sometimes took things too far.

Terry was also involved in that sad day at Oldham which resulted in the terraces at Hillsborough being closed for a while. He got sent off for something he didn't do and the fans went mad. I think it annoyed them so much because they liked him.

Whatever else I could write about Terry, I could never take away from him the fact he was a very good footballer for Sheffield Wednesday. Terry then left to join Sheffield United – he'll have to explain that one, along with a lot of other things!

Should be an interesting read . . .

JACK CHARLTON, England World Cup hero 1966 and Sheffield Wednesday manager 1977-1983

Introduction

REMEMBER me? I was a curly haired winger-cum-striker in football's 'golden days' of the 70s and 80s for a host of clubs starting at Doncaster Rovers and including Sheffield Wednesday, Everton, Forest, Southampton and Derby County.

They broke the mould when they made me. I lived and played hard, clashed with authority and always wanted to entertain the public when almost everyone else played safe. Call me a poor man's George Best; nobody could ever match the great man for style on or off the pitch but I was good, no doubt about that. Good enough to be spoken about as a future England player by Brian Clough and Jack Charlton, attract interest from great clubs such as Manchester United and Arsenal and play for Everton when they were at their very best. I even had a pop record in the charts and a fan club almost before they were invented.

Problem was I always made my life twice as hard as it should have been. That's why I have given this book the unusual title of *Regrets*. I walked out on possibly the greatest manager who ever lived; chucked in First Division football to play for my local team; became a Hillsborough legend in the famous Boxing Day massacre of Sheffield United only to get our ground closed due to a riot at Oldham Athletic; committed soccer and social 'suicide' by signing for the Blades; even did a Carlos Tevez years ahead of his time by refusing to play for one of the greatest teams of my generation at Everton. That's just the half of it. After a brief spell in Non League management, I staged a Reggie Perrin-style disappearance and quit the game I love for 16 long years.

As Bestie would have said, I spent a lot of time womanising and gambling (drinking was never my scene) – but wasted the rest! This book, like my football career, is a work of fact and entertainment. I trust it will keep you amused even if your football team has known better days. But it's more than that. As you get older, you get wiser – even me! Working on this, with the help of my ghostwriter John Brindley, has been a form of therapy. It has helped me to reflect on my life so far and admit my mistakes, almost too many regrets to mention. Even so, I can honestly say I've enjoyed 99 per cent of it!

I'll confirm the facts and dispel the many myths about some of the best known managers of my era – Cloughie, Tommy Docherty, Lawrie McMenemy, Jack Charlton and Howard Kendall – and tell you about my special friendship with the great Alan Ball. And I'll reveal more about some of the women I met along the way – the others I'll keep to myself, thank you!

You'll find me brutally honest, almost to a fault. I've never worried for long what people think about me or do to me, even when I got swindled out of a fortune! Hold your horses, folks, for the Terry Curran story – warts, romps, great goals, crushing disappointments and more. Enjoy the ride!

TERRY CURRAN, August 2012

1

Maverick in the Making

"THEY THINK it's all over . . ." Time stood still in the lounge of a council house in Kinsley, West Yorkshire, as Geoff Hurst fastened onto a clearance from Bobby Moore in the closing seconds of a thrilling World Cup final. Forty six years on I can still imagine Jack Charlton yelling Hurstie to hoof it and Alan Ball screaming 'pass it' in his distinctive squeaky voice. On and on Hurst trudged, as fast as his weary legs would carry him, before 100,000 fans at Wembley – plus eight brothers and one Dad in front of a small TV – exploded with relief and joy as he lifted that unforgettable shot high into the West German net.

"It is now . . ." Those great words from BBC commentator Ken Wolstenholme, a cousin on my Mum's side as it happens, sealed the greatest day in England's football history on July 30 1966 and also launched the dream of this young man. This 11-year-old wasn't interested in celebrating at a street party; I just wanted to grab a football and play with my brothers. My goal was to play for England, be on top of the world and make people happy – the way hat trick hero Hurstie, Bally and Big Jack had just done. A hell of an ask of a boy from a rugby-playing family and about to attend a comprehensive school where football wasn't even played – yet, it could, maybe should, have come true. I even had Big Jack and Bally roaring me on; amazingly they became two of my biggest supporters and it wasn't Germans or any opponents who stood in my way – but one very stubborn, hot headed individual called Edward 'Teddy' Curran!

I had the talent and the opportunities to work with five

of the best-known and, in some cases, best managers of my generation – and I blew it. Blew it big time! In my career, I went on my single-minded way, like Hurstie did that famous day, but blasted my final shot yards over the crossbar despite the advice of well meaning people ringing in my ears. Do I regret it? Yes, how else could I be writing a book with such a title? Did I enjoy it? Of course! Goals, girls and magic moments will live with me always – until the day the referee in the sky and his Russian linesman tells me it really is all over.

So let's go back to the start. I kicked off on March 20 1955 and, yes, my name really was – and is – Edward, not Terry. I was the seventh of eight brothers, born to a genuine couple praying for a daughter – a first hint you don't always get what you expect or ask for. Life was never easy after young John Curran, from Glasgow, visited Blackpool for a weekend and met and fell in love with a Yorkshire woman called Doris Batten. Pneumonia robbed my parents of their first child, Doreen, at the age of just two and they spent much of their married life trying unsuccessfully for another girl. Instead John arrived in 1942, followed by Peter and Terrence (not me, honestly!). More tragedy followed as their next child, Geoffrey, also died from pneumonia aged 18 months, before Alan, Bernard, David, Edward (that's me) and four years later Melvyn came on the scene.

A family of eight took some looking after, particularly in very difficult days. Mum had a succession of jobs – the last of which was in the bacon factory – to add to Dad's pay as a miner down the local pit. He didn't like it much, not many did – but the job simply had to be done and he never grumbled. Things got even worse when he had an accident at work that paralysed his arm and meant a long time off with no pay. My parents were proud to own their own house – a two up and two down terraced property bulging at the seams in Bond Street, Kinsley. David, Alan, Bernard and I huddled into one bed with the other lads in the second. We didn't complain as we knew no different. That was life. I'm not too sure even now how we got by.

Nobody had very much in the village – and what we had we shared. Neighbours handed down clothes and helped in whatever way they could. I got most of my gear second hand from my older brother David, just 18 months older and my sporting 'rival' for much of my childhood. He was just as crazy about football and we always argued over who was the better player. Problem was most villagers knew the answer: Dave had more skill, scored more goals and could so easily have made it as a professional player. After I signed for Cloughie at Forest, the great man invited him to the City Ground for a trial. But Dave turned him down because he only wanted to play local football. David was so good he bagged an incredible 208 goals one season, including his Sunday team! But he was happier enjoying his football and being a miner, so who is anyone to argue? To his great credit, David was never jealous about my professional career and backed me all the way. Today we're closer friends than ever. That's very important to me.

Time off from school in the summer was spent doing hard physical work in first the pea and then the potato fields as Alan, Bernard and David joined me in trying to put badly-needed cash into the family pot. The bus picked us up from the bottom of Wakefield Road in the village each weekday at 7.30am and took us – along with other young and willing Kinsley lads – to Ackworth, Featherstone and Castleford among other places. There I'd stay until about 2pm working flat out – short tea and lunch breaks apart – filling as many sacks as possible. Then we carried them on our shoulders to get them weighed and were paid ten shillings for each sack. It used to take about half-an-hour per sack, so I'd do about ten in every shift. This happened most days in my summer holidays from when I was eight until I was 15. We enjoyed the work, but the reason we and all the other lads did it was because our families needed the money. Brothers being brothers, there was always plenty of healthy competition to see who could fill the most sacks. I was quite good, but Bernard was quickest. When the pea season was over it was onto the potato fields until it was time to go back to school again.

Easier money was to be had down at the greyhound stadium in the village. The same brothers looked after the cars whilst the adults enjoyed the racing. The rule of thumb was this: the posher the vehicle, the more we were likely to be paid. Never have youngsters been so pleased to see a Zephyr or a Zodiac for which we might get five shillings – a modest Morris Miner, on the other hand, was worth 1d or 2d. Owner Jack Muggleston wouldn't allow us to watch the races but it was in our interests to stay until the very end at 10pm. Some car owners paid on entry, others waited until we'd done our jobs and were ready to drive off. If they didn't cough up at all, we'd do the vandals' work for them. Only joking, of course!

There wasn't a lot to do in the village: we had a co-op, barber's, betting shop, greengrocer, newsagent and post office plus a few pubs and clubs, including the Kinsley Hotel, Farmers' Working Men's Club and the Royal British Legion. Most interesting was a club called The Willow, owned by Jack Leach, the richest man in our world. He drove a Rolls Royce and hosted some very good singers, including Dame Shirley Bassey before she was famous. We're talking now, of course, about the swinging sixties with Elvis Presley, The Beatles and Rolling Stones and suddenly everyone was into their music, including young Teddy. For me, The Beatles were my idols – they never seemed to produce a bad record. Of the four brilliant young Scouse lads, the one who caught my imagination was John Lennon, talented, exciting and a true maverick. He had that unpredictable quality I particularly liked; no one knew what he was going to say or do next. Bernard was a Rolling Stones man, David worshipped The Kinks and Alan was a teddy boy. Between us, we got a good collection of records to satisfy our interests. In the long, hot summers, particularly on Sunday afternoons, people in the street kept their windows open and played their favourite music for all to hear and enjoy.

What made The Willow extra special was that Mum accommodated the artists when they came to perform. Usually, they'd come to our house to grab a few hours kip before the show, then return to sleep the night. I was introduced to a handsome young singer called Gerry Dorsey about to strut his stuff at The Willow. As most older readers will probably know already, I'm talking about the great Engelbert Humperdinck of *Release Me* and *Spanish Eyes* fame, not to mention the 2012 Eurovision Song Contest!

Generally, we made our own entertainment – there wasn't much else and anyway we were most at home with a football. Time came when the family was getting too big for the house and Mum and Dad had no choice but to give up our own property to move into a four-bedroom council house in nearby Tombridge Crescent. It was here that David and I started to slip down to the local football field to live out our fantasy. The only live football we watched – and a real treat it was too – was the FA Cup final. The earliest I can remember was the 1965 clash between Liverpool and Leeds United which the Reds won 2-1 with Ian St John, later the straighter half of Saint and Greavesie, on the scoresheet. But the one that meant most to me came 12 months later as Sheffield Wednesday faced Everton just a couple of months before the World Cup final. Although our closest professional club was Barnsley and Leeds had better support locally, I fell in love with the Owls that day – a love affair I will take to the grave. Maybe there was a hint of the nearly man of the future in it all as my team held and lost a two-goal lead, finally going down 3-2 after a double from an unknown called Mike Trebilcock.

David and I enjoyed watching FA Cup finals before going to the field to act out our own match. He was one team and I was the other; as a Chelsea fan, he pretended he was Peter Osgood and, as Manchester United were the other team in my young heart, I was George Best or Bobby Charlton. My love for United came from watching *Match of the Day*, which brought us most of our football. Of all their great players, the one I admired most and wanted to be like was Bestie. Who else? I loved the way he glided past defenders, the ball seemingly glued to his feet. He wasn't just a footballer, but an entertainer, showman, all-round super hero. Bestie played the way football should be played with flair and skill. Belonging to an era when most managers preached the exact opposite never changed that.

It was a great treat when Peter took me to my first ever visit to Old Trafford to watch United in a European Cup tie against AC Milan. The atmosphere was fantastic just being among thousands of excited people making our way into the stadium, let alone the match itself. United were the holders after Bestie inspired their 4-1 triumph against Benfica at Wembley. Although unable to defend their trophy, it was brilliant to see him and all my other heroes 'live'. Funnily enough the first professional game I'd been to was at Oakwell where Barnsley entertained Hartlepool. I remember being impressed with a skilful Scottish player called Alistair Miller, for Barnsley, playing in the old fashioned position of inside forward. More relevantly we stood close to the dugout a few yards from the Hartlepool manager, a young Brian Clough. Little did I know how famous Cloughie was going to become and that I would be a small part of his story.

The first of the brothers I looked up to was Peter. Watching him play in goal for Kinsley Boys was great fun. I stood on the touchline with some of my mates, Tony Wilson, Trevor Reece, Barry Steele, John O'Donald, Oliver Lewins, Ronnie McDonald and Barry Watson. My brother was a fantastic goalie and Barnsley wanted to sign him. But, again, all he wanted was to play local football – end of story. I learned a lot watching those village matches – they were frightening. Tackles flew in in a way you'd never see nowadays and how more lads didn't go home with broken legs I'm still not sure. But they gave me an idea how brave I needed to be to compete. David and I were the only young lads who played against the older age group in our village kick-abouts. One routine was the Sunday afternoon game when the lads came out of the pub after a few drinks. Nobody gave an inch to the scrawny little lad who regularly took liberties by trying to dribble past them, but the feeling between us all was great. Kinsley was a brilliant village where everyone knew everyone – the way things used to be.

When I was just eight years old, my family changed forever. Because I was so young, what happened took me completely by surprise but the older lads probably had more idea. There was always tension at home with eight brothers competing for attention in a limited space. But it hadn't been a happy place for some time with Peter and Terrence, both fiery teenagers, regularly coming to physical blows. That caused problems between Mum and Dad who had much different views on discipline. Dad was very quiet, rarely saying very much at all whilst Mum was the one whose word was law. If anyone got a belting it would be from Mum rather than Dad and they argued about how to deal with the warring brothers. Eventually it came to a head and Mum left the house for a few weeks. Probably trying to get some space, she moved down to London with a bloke called Alfie Smith. But she obviously got in touch because Terrence found out enough to go down south, bring Mum back home and give her new boyfriend a beating. The problems, however, didn't just go away and I was in for a real shock when the end finally came.

I was walking home up Tombridge Crescent when I saw Mum on the other side of the road wearing a black coat with a fur collar and carrying a little suitcase. "Where are you going?" I asked. "Don't worry, I will come back to see you," she said, giving me a kiss on the cheek. With that, she was gone! I hadn't a clue what she was talking about until Dad sat all the brothers down later that day and explained: "Your Mum and I have split up!" Blunt as that really. No explanation – just a raw shock and a hole in our lives that could never be filled. Put yourself in an eight-year-old's shoes and you can imagine how devastated and confused I felt. What next? What was my life going to be like now Mum was gone? Those were questions my young mind was never going to be able to answer however many times I chewed them over and over.

Mum leaving changed so many things. Yes, she visited once a week and Melvyn and I made the 12-mile trip each Saturday morning to Wakefield to see her. Of course, it was a nice feeling when she pulled up in her car, although we were less keen on spending time with her new man. Alfie was another quiet guy – even quieter than Dad if that was possible – and what happened wasn't his fault. He was ok to be honest but, back then, the only thing that mattered was that he wasn't Dad and never could be. He was the guy living with Mum, meaning my parents didn't look like getting back together.

Luckily, Mum had trained me well and I knew from an early age how to cook, iron and clean. The split meant I did those chores a lot more often. Although it was more usual for children to stay with their mother that was never likely to happen in our case. Perhaps it was the difficulty of finding a new home for eight brothers or splitting us up that made it impractical. It would also have been virtually impossible for a stepfather to take on such a large family. There was talk when the probation officer took an interest that some of us could go into care, but we resisted as strongly as possible. We just wanted to stay together.

Emotionally I was never the same kid. Mum was the one I'd go to when hurt, feeling ill or just upset. She'd have all the answers to satisfy me and put me back together again. Now she was gone and I didn't have that kind of support anymore. Dad did his level best and the brothers all pulled together but life changed for all of us. The subject of the split was a taboo. I honestly don't think it was ever discussed again but it was obvious to all of us Dad was heart-broken and that had a big influence on me as I became old enough to be interested in girls. I liked the idea of sex and having fun, but was never going to allow any female to get close enough to cause me the same upset. That lack of trust stayed with me for a lot of my adult life.

It wasn't a matter of taking sides although, as we all lived with Dad, we were bound to be more sympathetic with him. Life was hard, but that's what we expected. When I was about 10 or 11, I got up at 5am to do a milk round with David and Alan, getting back home by 7.30am to set off half-an-hour later for school. It was normal for big families to do such things in order to make ends meet. John, as the older brother, took the lead in keeping things together. The guy was brilliant to be honest. He always did everything humanly possible to ensure we made life tolerable for Dad and looked after each other. Even after he got married at the age of 21 and moved to Cudworth, he was still a great source of support. David, Melvyn, Bernard and me visited John and his wife Pam for Sunday lunch. I looked forward to the weekend to tuck into that juicy and tender pork. I loved it and can almost taste it now.

My first flirtation with professional football came when I was 12. David got selected to represent South Kirby Boys in a district match and, as Dad didn't like us to play in the same team as we were so competitive, I was supposed to be watching. I told him I'd bring my boots with me but he was adamant I shouldn't and checked the passenger's seat and the boot just to make sure. Yet I managed to smuggle them under the driver's seat. After all, there was always a slim chance one of our players would pull out. That's exactly what happened. The manager was one short so I volunteered to play. "But you haven't got your boots," Dad said. "Yes, I have," I said, scrambling inside the car to retrieve them. The game wasn't the greatest of successes as, if I remember, we got beat 18 goals to one! My consolation was I got the one and didn't do too badly. Being a district game, it attracted scouts and representatives from Aston Villa and Blackburn Rovers were there. Both picked me out as our best player and invited me for a trial. But Dad decided I was too young to be getting involved with a football club and that was the end of that.

Going to a rugby-playing school was another potentially big blow for a budding footballer. At least it reminded me that, had I followed family roots, I would have been a rugby league player. One of my relatives – my Mum's cousin Billy Batten – was a virtual legend. Not surprisingly, perhaps, he was not only a very talented wing and centre for Great Britain, England, Hunslet and Hull during the early 20th century but a maverick of his kind. He was so popular with Hull fans they printed 'Batten certain to play' over posters advertising home matches at The Boulevard and his benefit match in 1920 reaped a remarkable £1,079 13s 8d, very big money in his day. He was also known for his 'Batten Leap' as he hurdled tacklers, a trick he passed on to his son Eric, but was later banned because of its potential dangers.

Billy's other sons Bob and Billy Junior were also top class rugby league players as was Billy Junior's son, Ray, who played for Leeds, Great Britain and England. I had the pace and the natural bravery to become a rugby player. However my skinny teenage frame wasn't ideal for the rough and tumble of rugby – and, more to the point, I loved football! You could take football out of my timetable but no one could ever take it out of my heart.

I couldn't wait for the sports lesson, whether it was PE, tennis, athletics or football. I was a good all-round sportsman, enjoying tennis and table tennis and hinting at things to come in athletics. The school sports included a mile event for everyone, whatever their age. There was a handicap system with the younger ones such as me having a head start. For three successive years I made the most of it to finish first, displaying the same turn of speed that became so useful on the football field. I also showed the canny side to my nature at table tennis. We put a few quid on the outcome of our games and I had my eye on teaching this lad called Tony Poulson a lesson and making a profit. I was 14 and he was 18 and not a bad player, but I knew I was good enough to beat him. My policy as I played against other players was not to let him know what I could do. So I deliberately played badly and got beat until Tony came up to me and said he'd give me a game for a fiver and let me have five points start. Then it was gloves off and I showed my true colours to give him a good thrashing.

One of my first rants against authority came when I went to comprehensive school and marked their card about me and rugby. "I'm not playing that sport – not in your lessons, not for the school, not at all!" My message got through and I never had to – problem was I got banned from playing all the other school sports as well. That was a big blow as academic subjects never really interested me and school had always been about play as far as I was concerned. I loved to play two things – sport and truant! I'm not saying I was a bad truant but I had my moments. I remember being caught when I was 13 with my friends by the truant officer at the swimming baths in Wakefield. He would have reported me to my parents but I begged him to give me a second chance and, to his credit, he did. The fact I took a fair few beatings from my brothers and my Dad for skipping school, however, showed I used up plenty of my nine lives.

After the sports ban, I ticked off the days until I left school There was never any question of taking exams: I would get myself a job until I could fulfil my real dream. When it was my turn to give a short speech on leaving day, I spoke as I saw it: "I'm going to be a professional footballer!" I said. My teacher 'Killer' Graham didn't even try to hide his laughter. "Everyone wants to be a footballer, Teddy – try and think about other things." Dad, however, was more positive, telling me: "If that's what you really want to do, son, go for it." That was typical of a bloke who, although heartbroken by his broken marriage, continued to put others first.

The only other thing that ever interested was becoming a jockey. I'd always enjoyed watching horse racing – and still do – and at one time looked as if I would be about the right size. But, as I got steadily taller, that idea went out of the window. Oh and one other useful thing I did whilst at school – I became respectable with the lads by losing my virginity. 'It' happened when I was 15 years old and this girl was 13 – so you can understand why I won't mention her by name. Basically we'd grown up together at school but our first big moment, as with so many young people, wasn't quite the romantic triumph I'd been looking forward to.

Socially, I liked going to see the dogs at the greyhound stadium in Wakefield with my mate Clive Hulme. One night I thought our luck was really in as we had £100 in our pockets after the first four races. We couldn't lose! The next few races then went against us and we just had £20 left going into the last. Clive said we should leave the cash in our pockets to get the bus back home and still have a few bob to show for our night out but I was convinced I was onto a winner and eventually persuaded him to put all our money on a particular dog. Losing that bet not only meant we were clean out of cash but had to walk the 12 or so miles back from Wakey to the village. That gave us both plenty of time to curse our bad luck and for Clive to curse me – because that would have took a good few hours I can tell you! Yet that wasn't quite the end of the story. We got as far as Crofton, about halfway, when Clive said he couldn't walk a step further. That was when he suddenly took out a secret fiver from his sock and announced we would be calling a taxi. "Bloody hell," I said. "We could have put that money on the dog!"

Despite that, Clive helped me get my first job as an apprentice paint sprayer in Wakefield. We went together for an interview but there was a potential problem – there were two of us but only one vacancy. It didn't turn out to be an issue, however, as Clive, being a bit older, was none too impressed with wages of £4.50 a week. So the bloke offered me the job instead. For the next 18 months I got the bus at 7am each day to make the short journey to Wakey. That was four days a week with the other being spent at college in Leeds. I was on a three-year apprenticeship and enjoyed the work very much. It was a full-time job paying me money at a time when I was getting back into playing my football. I'd have probably stayed longer but for hearing that my mates were on £20 a week working on building sites. I then went to a factory packing items on a conveyor belt for £11 a week. At the end of each day my back was killing me and after a week I'd had more than enough. Given my wages, I told my supervisor I should be getting £11 a day and stick the job. From there, I took the plunge and went onto building sites where I was suddenly bringing in £40 a week, a fair proportion of which naturally went into the family budget.

Football-wise I got myself a spot playing for Kinsley Boys, an under 17s team, and soon found my form even though I hadn't played competitively for a couple of years. We were a good team, regularly winning leagues and cups, and when former Sunderland player George Mulhall invited us to The Shay to test our skills against a team of Halifax Town intermediates we taught them a lesson as well. We won that game 5-2 and I netted a hat trick. Mullall had seen enough in the young Curran to offer me a professional contract but that wasn't the end of the matter. The following week it was the turn of Doncaster Rovers to ask us to go to Belle Vue to play similar opposition and again I was among the goals tempting boss Maurice Setters to also offer me a trial. I'd given my word to Halifax and set off in a car with my friend Sammy Middleton and one of my brothers with every intention of signing at The Shay. But it was a fairly lengthy journey and about halfway there I got cold feet and asked them to turn back. As soon as I got home, I rang Setters and told him I'd love to come for a trial. Donny were a struggling Fourth Division club and Halifax were in the Third; also I was only being guaranteed a trial instead of a contract – yet there was one very important thing in Donny's favour. The town was only 20 miles away, so I could commute rather than leave home. Also, I had enough confidence in my ability to believe I could convince Setters to offer me terms – and enough cheek to go back to Mullall cap in hand if I didn't!

It was a big call in a number of ways and Dad didn't agree with my decision. He pointed out that Halifax was the sensible choice as they were the only ones making a concrete offer but there was no talking me out of what I wanted to do. Remember I was giving up my job on a building site on the best money I'd earned so far in my young life to go for a trial for which I wouldn't even get any expenses and with no guarantee of anything to show for it. I was also given no idea how long the trial would last. Typically, despite his misgivings, Dad went out of his way to give me every chance. He worked his night shift down the pit, and then got up in the morning to take David to work and Melvyn to school before driving me to Donny for the football. He slept in his car whilst I was there before going back to cook tea before leaving for work again for a 9pm start. It all lasted for more than two months. I was the one on trial but Dad worked hardest, knowing I couldn't get there without him. There's no written guarantee when you follow your dream – however long you've yearned for it – that it will happen. Around the same time as I was going into football, my great mate Clive Hulme set out to become a jockey but was thrown off a horse virtually straightaway and went back into 'normal' work. I was to be one of the lucky ones.

These days I'd probably have come through the academy but here I was basically coming off the streets with very little football behind me and training with Doncaster's first team squad. As the first week or two went by, I guessed I must be doing something right as I was mixing with seasoned professionals such as Graham Moore, a Welsh international who had played for Manchester United and Charlton Athletic; John Haselden, an experienced player with his home town club; and Alan Murray, who joined us from Brentford. For a lad who enjoyed nothing more than making defenders, particularly older ones, look foolish that meant potential bother. After one such move, Moore turned to me and said, if I ever did that to him again, he'd give me a 'clip'. He meant it, too, but at least it was a sign I was winning his respect. Moore was one of the most competitive people I came across in my whole career, both in the five-a-sides in training and on the pitch. I took to him instantly because he was always cracking funny jokes and sharing stories about famous players like Bobby Charlton and Bestie he'd played with at Old Trafford – my idols, so I was very impressed. John also taught me an important lesson, although I was far too young and naive to realise it. A rugged defender, he was about 30 years old but, watching him struggle to get out of the bath and hobble along, seemed more like 65. I took the mickey and he took it in good heart. But he told me: "You wait until you're 30, you won't be laughing then!" As a teenager, I thought he was talking rubbish and I'd never be as bad as that. He was right: I was worse!

Just what was at stake for me was brought home by a surprise night out organised by my friends Oliver Lewins, Trevor Reece and Chalkie White. They picked me up from Donny and I expected they were going to take me home. When we got onto the motorway I realised we were going in a different direction altogether and asked where we were heading. "Anfield," said Oliver. "We're going to see our Cyril play!" He was talking about Cyril Knowles, one of two young brothers from our neighbouring village of Fitzwilliam who were making it big in the game. In fact the area was becoming quite a hot bed for sporting talent with Cyril and Peter Knowles, friends of my brothers Peter and Terrence, starring for Spurs and Wolves, John Radford, from Hemsworth, being a key member of Arsenal's League and FA Cup double winning side in 1971 and South Kirkby's Eric Probert, playing for Burnley. That's not to mention the best known of them all, England and Yorkshire cricket legend Geoffrey Boycott, a native of Fitzwilliam.

Spurs lost 3-0 that night as I witnessed the might of Bill Shankley's Liverpool machine in action – little did I think a few months later I'd be playing against them! I enjoyed watching Cyril, a fantastic attacking left back who would have won far more than his four England caps had it not been for being in competition with Leeds United's Terry Cooper. I got to know the guy, who inspired the song *Nice One Cyril* quite well during my career before he very sadly passed away through cancer at the age of 47. His brother Peter, by the way, was perhaps even more talented, being capped at England Under 23 level and scoring goals by the bucketful at Wolves before giving up football in 1970 to become a Jehovah's Witness. Each to their own, as they say!

Me being me I took the odd liberty in my early days at Donny. I was picked to play in an intermediate game at Mansfield Town on the same day Kinsley Boys had an important cup tie against Toll Bar – a game I didn't want to miss. I couldn't do both. Or could I? I also remember it well because it was Grand National day and I had £20 on Crisp to win. It was that fantastic race everyone remembers when Crisp led for almost the whole race at Aintree only to be overtaken by Red Rum in the final straight. That amazing triumph made both horse and owner Ginger McCain famous as Red Rum, ridden by Brian Fletcher, trailed by 30 lengths at one stage – and 15 coming to the last fence – and still overtook my bet. I was never that lucky at the bookies.

Anyway, Dad and my best friend Clive Hulme took me to Mansfield for an 11am kick off. I was in the starting line up and played the first 45 minutes before telling the coach I was struggling with an ankle knock and would have to come off. Dad and Clive then took me to Toll Bar at Bentley for the Kinsley cup tie thinking I was going to watch my brother David. That game kicked off at 3pm and Dad, not for the first time, wasn't expecting me to play. "I thought you were injured," he said. "Don't worry, Dad, I'm feeling a lot better now!" I replied. I was luckier at football than I was at the races as I played in our 3-2 victory and nobody at Rovers was any the wiser.

I was pleased with how things were going at Rovers but, as weeks turned into months, I still had no firm indication whether they wanted me. Then came the chance to play in a midweek reserve game at Sunderland. There must have been 2,500 or 3,000 there, more than an average first team match at Belle Vue. They hadn't come to watch me or any of the Donny lads but had turned up to get their tickets for the 1973 FA Cup final just three days later against mighty Leeds United at Wembley. I had a really good evening, giving their left back Chris Guthrie quite a chasing. Afterwards fellow Donny players were quick to congratulate me on how well I'd played, pointing out that Guthrie was in line to play in the big match. As it turned out the game proved a success for both of us with Guthrie doing a good job marking Peter Lorimer as Bob Stokoe's defence kept a clean sheet to help pull off one of the great FA Cup shocks through a single goal from Ian Porterfield (more about him later!). Just how big an influence my performance had in his decision I'm not sure but Maurice Setters sat me down a few days later and uttered the words all football-mad youngsters long to hear: "I'm offering you a contract!" Elated, thrilled, excited – all those words couldn't quite describe quite how I felt. Another young footballer was coming off the Kinsley production line!

2

'Teddy' of the Rovers

OPENING my first wage packet as a professional footballer could have brought me back down to earth. It contained just £20, half of what I'd been earning on the building site. But, honestly, that didn't bother me. I'd have happily signed my two-year contract for nothing just to call myself a proper footballer.

Donny were down on their luck. Annual strugglers against relegation from Division Four – and therefore the entire Football League – they never had more than a couple of pennies to rub together. To save a little cash, Setters delayed officially taking me on until July 1 so they didn't have to pay me. So I was sent down the building site again as a couple of the club's directors were in the trade. There was method in their madness – hard manual work would build up the skinny teenager. But they didn't know I was a rebel. We were working in this two up two down house and I dug up the floor using my hand pick – bloody hard work! I was pleased with what I'd done but, after my gaffer had taken a look, the big gaffer was called in and said: "It's not right; you're going to have to dig it up again!" When this was repeated some time later and the gaffer-in-chief rudely ordered me to do it for a third time I snapped. I told him to take his pick and stick it where the sun don't shine (or something similar) and that stroppy outburst was the end of me on the building site! Luckily, Setters agreed it was time for me to play some football, which was what I'd signed up for.

I was lucky to be quickly taken under the wing of one of the top players in the Donny side, big striker Brendan

O'Callaghan. For some reason, Brendan treated me like a younger brother which was a great help in me settling into the club. A commanding figure at about 6'3" or 6'4", Bren was a great guy with more O levels to his name than a normal squad of footballers. If anyone gave me any trouble, he took on the role of Big Brother and sorted them out. We shared the same digs run by landlady Mrs Norbury with Alan Murray, who was four or five years older than me. Although different in almost every way, we all got on very well. Alan was a king of the one-liners, Brendan, the straight guy and I, a typical healthy 18-year-old taking his first steps in the professional game and seeking a good time off the field.

Alan, who later assisted Graeme Souness at both Blackburn Rovers and Newcastle United, used to buy a monthly porno mag called *Knave*. Meanwhile Brendan was a good Catholic and photos of undressed women weren't my scene either as I preferred the real thing. But it gave us all a few laughs. Alan didn't want to be found with the magazine when Mrs Norbury's daughter came round to clean, so hid it under my bed! Sure enough she found it and I got a right telling off from Mrs Norbury who took a lot of convincing the magazine wasn't mine. She was all for reporting me to the manager who didn't take any nonsense. Alan and Brendan enjoyed the moment to the full but eventually the good woman believed my side of the story.

Clashing lifestyles also caused the odd minor problem or two with Brendan. Like a lot of footballers, I found it difficult to come down from the excitement of playing a match. So rather than rest I went out on a Saturday night to a nightclub on the airfield near Belle Vue until the early hours of Sunday morning. Even at 2am or 3am I still wasn't ready to turn in, so found an all-night coffee bar before returning to Mrs Norbury's between 5am and 6am. Big Bren was a totally different kettle of fish, staying in on a Saturday night. We were both Catholics, the difference being he took his religion seriously enough to actually go to church. So he'd wake me up at about 7am to ask whether I was coming with him to Mass and I'd be as polite as someone who'd only been in bed for an hour or so could. I had something much more urgent to do – sleep!

Donny Rovers were a strange mixture. Looking at some of the names in that squad, including Peter Kitchen, Mickey Elwiss, Brendan and Stephen Elliott, we could have been a good side. We also had promising young lads such as Stan Brookes and Stephen Read who never quite made the most of their potential. We could certainly score goals but, if we scored four, our opponents would probably score five! Defence? We didn't have one. The bloke with the most difficult job of all was goalkeeper Kim Book, brother of Tony, the former Manchester City legend. Mind you, he was used to being in the firing line having kept goal for Northampton that famous day when Bestie returned from a six-week suspension to score six in an 8-2 United victory in the FA Cup. Partly out of mischief and also because I was a huge George Best fan, I joined others in taking the mickey out of Kim and asking him everything we could about the game. He told me the great man sold him so many dummies he went in about three directions for one of the goals.

I'll never forget my Football League debut. I'd been doing reasonably well in training but it was still a very special moment when the boss told me on the Friday I was playing at Gillingham the following day – Saturday, September 29 1973. We set off on our long journey to Kent in the team bus at 7am on the morning of the game. My mate Gary Oakley was keen to come and watch my debut and, as I'd just passed my driving test, I loaned him my first car, a Morris Minor I'd paid £200 for about a month previously.

As a lad I'd always played as an out and out striker but Setters picked me on the right wing, a position that stuck for a good deal of my career. I can understand why he and successive managers thought that way – they could see I had pace and liked to take on defenders. But, for me, playing wide always seemed like a trap. If I stayed wide and the game bypassed me, I'd get flak and, if I moved inside to try to get more involved, I was told I wasn't in my right position. But, yes, I always enjoyed the thrill of taking on my marker although sometimes I used to beat him two or three times before crossing the ball!

On my first day, however, the Gills were all over us like a rash and, although I didn't think I played that badly, there wasn't much I could do to prevent a 5-1 thrashing. Setters went barmy afterwards although I was too green to know whether his criticisms were right or wrong. It couldn't get any worse, you might think, but it did! Gary came up to me afterwards looking sheepish and said: "It's been a bad day!"

"Yes, I know, we've got beat 5-1," I answered.

"No, worse than that, I didn't put any oil in your car and it seized up as I got into Gillingham!"

Being the laid back character I am, I wasn't angry with Gary even though my prized first vehicle had to be towed to the scrapyard. He made his own way back home that day but we remain good friends even now.

My debut made the local newspaper headlines and I was also mentioned in positive terms the following Saturday when I took my home bow in the 3-1 victory over Peterborough United. This was probably the first time the world had heard of 'Terry' Curran. Christened 'Edward', I was known to everyone in my world as Teddy – that's except Donny's assistant manager, Johnny Quigley, who played for Nottingham Forest in their 1959 FA Cup Final victory over Luton Town. He told the newspapers my name was Terry and there was nothing I could do about it. I remember talking to Joe Slater, one of the local Doncaster journalists, and telling him straight that Terry wasn't my name. "Well, it sounds a lot better than Teddy!" he replied. Who was I to argue?

I did well enough to keep my new name in the frame as I played a fair number of league games before Christmas as Donny struggled for survival. New Year's Day 1974 saw us celebrate by going to the bottom of the league despite getting a 2-2 draw with Yorkshire rivals Bradford City. That didn't matter too much for the whole town was buzzing with FA Cup fever. Victories over two modest opponents may not have promised much but this year was different. Poor Donny, 92nd and bottom of the whole Football League, were drawn against the team at the very top, Bill Shankley's Liverpool, at fortress Anfield, where they'd remained unbeaten during the first half of the season. That week you couldn't go anywhere without people talking about the cup tie. The clash was such a home banker I'd have happily had a tenner on Donny – if I had one! I was just excited to be involved in any way. I was substitute and sat on the bench next to Setters, my eyes drawn to the great Shankley as he organised his all-star team including Phil Thompson, Steve Heighway, Ian Callaghan, Emlyn Hughes, Ray Clemence – and a wee Donny lad by the name of Kevin Keegan.

Keegan was just beginning to make his mark after his dream move from Scunthorpe United and almost inevitably put Liverpool in front after just three minutes. Picking the ball out of his net so early, Bookie must have wondered whether this was going to be Manchester United all over again. Nobody would have been surprised had Liverpool gone on to win by five or six. Yet, incredibly, just 15 minutes later we were in front. Our equaliser came after six minutes when the mighty Clemence fumbled from Peter Woods, a midfielder we got from Manchester United, and Peter Kitchen toe poked us back into the game. If that wasn't enough, Mrs Norbury's dream team then combined to give us a 2-1 lead. Murray's cross evaded a series of Reds and there was Brendan at the far post to shoot home. It took some believing but there was nothing lucky about it. We continued to cause Liverpool problems as the first half came to a close although we did have one escape when Thompson rapped a header against the bar.

Setters tried to keep us sane as the excitement among the lads was incredible. He knew Liverpool would come at us like an express train in the second half with their famous fans roaring them on. He told us to frustrate them, keep our lead and our heads for as long as possible and the home fans would start to get anxious. My only disappointment was we were doing so well it was difficult to see me getting a game. Liverpool fans are some of the fairest you'll find anywhere and gave our Donny lads a rip-roaring reception when we went back onto the field. We deserved it, too, for we'd played some great stuff. Sitting next to Setters, the tension and excitement mounted by the minute. All was going to plan as we kept our noses in front and Liverpool fans began to get on their heroes' backs. Setters turned to me and said: "I want Manchester United away in the next round!" But after 57 minutes it was 2-2 thanks to that man Keegan again – Callaghan supplied the cross and Donny's favourite son scored his second of the game.

Everyone expected Liverpool to win it from there and they piled on the pressure with Peter Cormack having one shot cleared off the line. But we still had our chances and full back Alec Lindsay had to do the same thing to prevent Steve Wignall edging us back in front. What happened next could so easily have caused one of the most famous FA Cup moments of all time. With just a couple of minutes left, Kitchen lobbed the ball over the England goalkeeper and the whole of Anfield held its breath. It looked set for the back of the net – and certain Donny victory – but instead hit the bar and rebounded out to Emlyn Hughes, or old Crazy Horse, as they called him. Even then, Hughes, in his panic, headed his attempted clearance against the bar and over again. What a moment, what a match! Legend has it that John Ryan, later the chairman who so magnificently transformed Donny's fortunes from Non League strugglers to a respectable Championship club, was behind the goal where that last gasp incident took place. Can't be right – John would have sucked the ball in!

Nevertheless the town was rocking with the unlikely thought of the best team in England coming to Belle Vue for an FA Cup replay. These were the difficult days of Ted Heath's 3-day week with power cuts and the like and Donny nearly beating Liverpool was a fantastic boost for morale. I was just hoping I'd get a kick in the second match played at some unearthly time the following Tuesday afternoon to get over the problem of using the lights.

Belle Vue, Donny's much-loved ground before they switched to the Keepmoat a few seasons ago, was, like the team itself, full of contradictions. It was old, creaky and almost falling apart at the seams – yet created an almost unique atmosphere on the very rare occasions when full. It seemed like the whole of Doncaster got the afternoon off to see if we could complete the shock result of the century. Officially there were 22,000 there – about ten times our normal home gate. They were hanging from the pylons and from every possible vantage point both inside and outside the old ground. This was a sell-out and then some as excitement was at fever pitch.

Setters handled the situation well by only telling me an hour before kick off I was in the side. He probably thought that would be the best way of managing a teenager's nerves but he needn't have worried as I was ready to give as good as I got. I was already getting used to worldly-wise full backs giving me the verbals and Alec Lindsay greeted me with a warning that he'd break my leg if I got too near him. "Bring it on," I replied. "Next time the ball comes, I'll give you some back!" As a lad who'd grown up as one of eight brothers I'd learned a lot of things, including the need to look after myself and fight back. I never lacked confidence and knew I could handle myself if need be. That explains why, although I never got sent off at Donny, I picked up my share of bookings, mostly for retaliation. Predictably, the game and our hopes disappeared in a blur and I can't remember a lot about the following 90 minutes. Perhaps I was still dazed after a memorable encounter with England goalkeeper Ray Clemence. I went into a challenge with the great man, collided with his shoulder and bounced back about 10 yards outside the penalty area! Again, we played quite well but, as so often on these occasions, the higher-rated side came out on top at the second time of asking as Liverpool won 2-0. The Reds went on to lift the FA Cup itself in style when they brushed aside Malcolm MacDonald and Newcastle United 3-0 in a very one-sided final yet we could so easily have knocked them out at their first hurdle.

Our fantastic efforts against Liverpool didn't mean much when we came back to the bread and butter of scrapping for our Football League survival. Just four days later we lost 2-1 at home to Brentford and, with Workington and Chester City also winning at Belle Vue and Reading giving us a five-goal thrashing, we were well and truly rooted to the bottom of the league with matches running out. We desperately needed a lift and I helped to provide one in our next home match against Scunthorpe United when my run past two men was halted by a scything tackle and Alan Murray won the game from the penalty spot.

Tuesday, March 22 1974, two days after my 19th birthday, was a big night for me. The visit of promotion-chasing Newport County was always going to be an important game for us as we had just closed the gap between ourselves and our fellow strugglers with a 2-1 victory in the South Yorkshire derby at Rotherham United. The early signs weren't too promising though. The game was scheduled for 5.30pm and the crowd of 1,163 was the lowest in the club's history. The match was no great shakes although I went close with a header – yes, a header! – in the first half. Graham Moore was leading the attack with Peter Higgins and me on the flanks and we gradually got our game going after the break. Higgins put us in front and then in the 73rd minute came my big moment. The local press reported I scored my first senior goal with a coolly-taken close range effort – I'll take their word for it because I don't remember too much about the detail. It was, however, a great moment for me, all the more so as our 2-0 victory lifted us to within a point of the second from bottom side. I was so high I didn't even mind getting booked for an incident I wasn't even involved in.

Our problems were far from over as we then went three games without scoring and were still bottom of the pile going into the last six fixtures. A 3-3 draw against Lincoln City at Sincil Bank finally moved us up a place and a happy Easter then saw us play the same opponents at Belle Vue just 24 hours later. I started the match in midfield but got much more joy when I moved up front and went on to have one of my best games yet for Donny creating a number of chances. Peter Woods put us in front and big Brendan did what he did best as we celebrated a vital 2-0 victory. We even had thoughts of getting out of the bottom four altogether as then we saw off Northampton Town 2-1 at Belle Vue with me getting the late winner for my second senior goal. But we then lost the return match against the Cobblers and at Mansfield in our 46th and final game to finish third from bottom on 35 points. There was relief all round as we were re-elected after what had been a very difficult season for the club – but a very exciting one for me as I'd experienced the highs of playing in the Football League for the first time and the never-to-be-forgotten Liverpool experience.

My second season with Rovers was similar with the side struggling near the bottom of the table almost from the off. Again, we had the annoying habit of scoring plenty of goals, but conceding a fair few more. With the bottom four teams having to apply for re-election to the Football League, we seemed almost certain to be going cap in hand to our fellow clubs again when after 30 games we had managed only five victories. Even when we scored four goals away to Shrewsbury at Gay Meadow, the journey home proved a disappointing one as we managed to leak seven. Again I had the consolation of being among the Donny scorers. We knew we were in trouble but it still came as a shock when the manager explained that he was leaving Belle Vue. He had tears in his eyes as he explained his unusual departure. He wasn't sacked, but was suspended, or put on gardening leave as they put it these days, with no one knowing anything about the circumstances other than our poor results. I was bound to take it worse than most as Setters had been the guy who had given me my first contract, selected me for my league debut and had sufficient confidence to make the teenager a regular in his side. But it softened the blow a great deal that the club then brought in Stan Anderson, a man I also got on particularly well with, to take over on a caretaker basis.

Stan immediately set about organizing us better and making us into a much more difficult side to beat. His impact was amazing as we soon went on a run of five successive victories – something Donny fans could only dream about. During this spell, Brendan O'Callaghan and Peter Kitchen, who became almost Belle Vue legends, started to hit it off really well as a partnership up front with me supplying the ammunition from the wing. It all started with a 3-0 home victory over Torquay United in which I got myself a goal before we went to Oakwell and beat rivals Barnsley by the only goal – a result sure to make the new boss an instant hero. Mansfield made the short journey for the second of two high-scoring matches, with Donny nicking a seven-goal thriller and yours truly on the scoresheet. By the time we had gone to Newport County and won 2-0 and repeated the scoreline against Northampton at Belle Vue, we were well on the way to dragging ourselves clear of trouble. In the end we finished in 17th place with 40 points and our place in the Football League was secure for another season. An added bonus that campaign was the chance to play against a Manchester United XI managed by Tommy Docherty in a friendly. The United side may have consisted of reserve and youth team players, but it was still a thrill to play against a side representing my boyhood heroes, especially as I managed to score the winning goal in the final seconds.

More importantly for my career I was gaining a reputation as a young winger of promise. The local press was raving about a young player who wasn't afraid to take on his marker and try the unexpected. There was no doubt in my mind where I was heading – the First Division. From my first game, my goal was to make it big in the game and clubs started to take notice of me during that second season. Sometimes lads lose focus when a move to a bigger club is possible but for me it was the perfect reason to get my head down and work still harder. I wanted to make damned sure they noticed me! It still came as a shock, however, when I went home one day and Dad told me some very interesting news. "You're not going to believe who has been on the phone for you today," he teased. "First, it was Don Revie – then Brian bloody Clough!" You can only imagine what a boost it was for a youngster in the Fourth Division to be interesting two of the greatest managers of the era.

I had great respect for what Revie achieved at Elland Road. His Leeds of the early 1970s was the best club side I've ever seen and that includes Arsene Wenger's Arsenal when they went through a complete Premier League season unbeaten in 2003-04. Mesmerising footballers Eddie Gray, Johnny Giles and Peter Lorimer played incredible stuff, without getting the legacy they deserved. In my view they would have given the great Brazilian World Cup team of 1970 a run for their money – they really were that good. Revie phoned me a couple of times and asked whether I'd be interested in playing for Leeds United, still a major force in the First Division. "Who wouldn't want to play for Leeds?" was my instant answer. And I meant it. What happened to Leeds' interest, however, I'm not really sure. Perhaps they were put off by the fee but things never got beyond that initial stage.

Ironically, one reason Leeds were never lauded – or even liked – by supporters outside Yorkshire was the very public dislike of Mr Clough. It's one of the best documented stories in football how Cloughie blasted Revie's side whilst at Derby, then continued to do exactly the same thing when he got the job during 44 bizarre days at Elland Road. By the time

Cloughie's interest had turned into something more concrete, the great man had found a new home beside the River Trent at sleepy Nottingham Forest. He sent his scouts out to see me in action three times for Donny Rovers. Then he sped down the motorway – a little too quickly as he got nicked by the police on route! – just in time for the second half of a match at Barnsley.

Cloughie also phoned a couple of times to ask if I was interested in joining Forest. You bet I was. "Don't go signing for anyone else, young man!" he ordered. Then he told me he wouldn't be phoning again but my contact at Forest would be a scout called Maurice Edwards. I was coming towards the end of my two-year deal at Donny and Anderson was quick to offer me another one, increasing my wages by £20 per week. Cloughie knew all about this and dealt with it in an interesting way. He told me not to commit myself to a new contract and would ensure I didn't miss out financially. Each week Edwards travelled over to hand me the extra £20. The first time we met was in a fish and chip shop and after that at The Crown Hotel in nearby Bawtry. Of course this wasn't a legal way of going about things but was fairly typical of football at the time. I was just grateful for the extra cash and still excited by the fact a manager I rated in the Bill Shankley class was so interested in bringing me to Forest.

Cloughie's approach became the subject of a *News of the World* front page article some years later when the newspaper was trying to dig up as much dirt as it could on him in the light of the Teddy Sheringham affair and the alleged money in a brown envelope when the striker was transferred from Forest to Spurs. I was caught on the hop as I was at a racecourse when the call came and didn't fully realise the significance of it. It's a common problem dealing with journalists that, unless you're fully switched on, you're not always sure where they are going with their questions. All I did was tell them the truth that Cloughie's lot had paid me what seemed like a small amount of money to ensure I didn't re-sign for Donny.

I never have had any intention of dropping either Cloughie in it or Edwards, a grand old chap I still know to this day. I never heard anything back from Cloughie after the story – he was probably too used to making headlines to be unduly bothered. I hope so because the last thing I wanted to do was to hurt him,

Signing for Forest was nothing like a done deal – at least in Anderson's eyes, who told me of interest from Everton manager Harry Catterick and Ken Furphy at Sheffield United. There'd also been reports of Tottenham Hotspur checking my progress. There was just time for me to start a third season with Donny. Anderson was now in permanent control with Setters officially being sacked in the July before eventually winning his case for unfair dismissal. I was pleased to round off my Donny career with two goals in a 2-2 draw at Tranmere Rovers. My last contribution in a Rovers shirt was to score the equaliser with a fierce shot just a couple of minutes from time. I couldn't have thought of a better way of signing off. A meeting was then arranged in Nottingham and Anderson told me on the way not to sign a contract at the City Ground because he'd fixed up appointments with both Everton and Sheffield United. What Anderson didn't know as we turned up at a bed and breakfast owned by Forest official Alan Hill to meet Cloughie was that he'd been courting me for six months and my mind was pretty well made up. Needless to say, Stan was none too pleased about Forest's conduct when he found out some time later exactly what had been going on behind his back.

Cloughie wasn't in any doubt, greeting me with the words: "young man, you are signing for the champions!" I told him I'd sign for Forest on one condition – I was in the side on Saturday. "No problem, you're in," said Cloughie. He asked how much money I wanted and I said £60 a week. "I'll pay you £90," he answered. I should have asked for £500 by that score! But, honestly, the money didn't matter; I just wanted to play for Brian Clough. The great man seemed just as keen.

"We have finally got you – we've been chasing you for six months," he said. "Now I'll make you into an England player." "Don't bother," I replied. "I'll do that myself." I wasn't short of confidence, you see, and that was one thing Cloughie liked about me.

I was valued at £75,000 in the deal – big money in those days – and was pleased Donny, who'd treated me so well, got plenty out of it. In return, they signed Ian Miller, a replacement winger who went on to do very well at Donny, and goalkeeper Darren Peacock, who also became a very popular figure in South Yorkshire playing more than 300 games in two spells. As for me, leaving the club and the people who were good enough to give me my first chance in professional football was sad, particularly as it was full of friendly, genuine football folk. I'm thrilled that, after taking big steps backwards when Ken Richardson became one of the most notorious chairmen of all time, Doncaster Rovers have now become such a credit to the area and to football since John Ryan took over. They have always had a place in my heart and I'm more than happy my career has now gone full circle and I'm part of the team at the Keepmoat coaching Donny's players of the future at their Centre of Excellence.

Back then, however, my mind was clear – I had a chance to play for one of the game's greatest managers and couldn't wait to get started.

3

Playing for Cloughie

"Terry Curran made an impact when he first joined Forest. Even in those days he was a bit of a rarity as a genuine winger, who had loads of pace and could beat defenders. I remember all his big thick curly hair falling out as a reaction to the flu jab – I refused it myself after that! Then he started our Second Division promotion season with an outstanding personal performance at Fulham. Terry was making a good contribution to Forest when he suffered a serious injury against Burnley – but for that who knows what he could have achieved under Brian Clough?"

John McGovern, captain of Nottingham Forest's European Cup winning sides 1979 and 1980

CHAMPIONS? Bloody hell, Forest weren't even the best team in Nottingham when I walked through the door.

Fans were tiring of hearing about the club's heyday in the mid-1960s when a side containing Ian Storey-Moore, Henry Newton, Terry Hennessey and Frank Wignall finished second only to a George Best-inspired Manchester United in the First Division. Relegated in 1971-72, they didn't look like bouncing back any time soon as first Matt Gillies, then Dave Mackay and Allan Brown had taken charge. Worse still for the supporters, they had to sit back and watch as Cloughie and then Mackay himself led Derby to two First Division titles. There'd been a burst of new optimism and enthusiasm when Cloughie first breezed through the door of a tired-looking City Ground in January 1975 but even that had been a false dawn as they stumbled to 16th spot in the Second Division at the end of his first mini-season. Good job I wasn't short of confidence!

I told chairman Brian Appleby I would get his club promotion – a bold promise from a teenager who'd played all his football in the Fourth Division. Nevertheless Appleby, a nice bloke from a legal background, was impressed enough to promise he'd buy me a suit if I came up with the goods. He was such a good guy he later bought me one anyway even though we were still a long way off the First Division.

My introduction to Forest left me amazed and, for a very rare time in my life, almost speechless. On the day I signed, the Reds were at home to Rotherham United in a League Cup tie and Cloughie invited me to stay and watch my new team in action. I was in the stand as Forest won 5-1 before the manager invited me to go down to the dressing room afterwards to meet the lads. Understandably, Cloughie was in a very good mood after seeing his side play so well and greeted me like royalty. He took me up to Martin O'Neill, who'd had a fine game on the right side of Forest's midfield, and said: "Martin, I'd like to introduce you to the young man who will be taking your place on Saturday!" I didn't know where to put myself and that's before I had any idea what a strong character O'Neill was. That was typical Cloughie but not fair on either of us. It certainly didn't help me settle in at Forest. Although the lads, O'Neill included, always talked with me, I didn't get off to the best start socially with my new team mates and felt a bit of an outsider for several months. But it did confirm one thing about Cloughie – if he made a promise, he'd do his very best to keep it.

Despite their modest fortunes on the field, Forest had the X-Factor neither Everton nor Sheffield United could match. It wasn't the lure of all those gorgeous girls in Nottingham, where females were supposed to outnumber males three to one according to local folklore – but the guy in the manager's seat. It's well worth remembering when you consider Forest's incredible exploits at home and in Europe in the following few years that the nucleus of Cloughie's great side was there from day one at the City Ground. Quite a lot of the squad had been there for some time – another reason why I struggled to become one of the in-crowd. Viv Anderson, Martin O'Neill, John Robertson, Ian Bowyer, Garry Birtles and Tony Woodcock were all destined to become household names and winners of European Cup medals – but you would never have guessed it. They'd all, with the exception of Birtles, been in and out of the Forest side without pulling up any trees. The magic of Cloughie was getting the very best out of his players and blending them into a team much stronger than the sum of its parts. That's not to say some of them hadn't got genuine talent.

Viv, known as 'Spider' to Forest fans because of his long, gangly legs, was an extremely good defender, who thoroughly deserved to become the first black player to win a full England cap. He had fantastic pace to win his battles on the right side of Forest's defence and quick reading of the game to cover for the central defenders. Viv, along with Bert Bowery – a man mountain you'd never mess with off the field but much softer on it – were two black players in the Forest side at a time when there weren't all that many in the Football League. Bowery only played a handful of first team matches but Viv was a regular and took terrible racial abuse from opposition players and fans. There'd be monkey chants and bananas thrown onto the pitch which was awful for Viv and very uncomfortable for the rest of the Forest lads. It didn't help that our fans hurled similar abuse when we were playing against black lads. It's almost unthinkable today that was allowed to happen. All players, whatever their colour, background or creed, should naturally be treated with respect but that wasn't the case back in the day.

Woody, too, was exceptional, although Cloughie was slower to appreciate him. I remember travelling to Bristol City for a league game when Cloughie asked me who had been our best player in the previous night's reserve game against Manchester United. When I quickly answered Martin O'Neill,

Cloughie said: "That just shows me you know nothing about football." I stood my ground. "Martin was our best player," I said. "And I'll tell you another thing – you shouldn't even be thinking of selling Tony Woodcock because he's a really good player." Woody had failed to establish himself in the Forest first team and, having had loan spells at Lincoln City and Donny, didn't look to have a future at the club. In fact it was rumoured that, if Rovers could have scraped together £20,000, they would have snatched a striker who was later to star for Forest, FC Cologne, Arsenal and England. Cloughie, naturally, didn't admit I was right – but when he got a measure of Woody's talent he played a key role in developing him into the player he later became.

Robbo, however, was the player! Alongside Peter Shilton, who came just as I was leaving, he was the only member of Forest's trophy-winning team deserving of the word 'great' – and that includes the game's first £1m man Trevor Francis. Yet when I arrived, he didn't look the part. He was always scruffily dressed in clothes looking like they'd never seen the same wardrobe. You'd see him shuffling along in a blue suit and beige hush puppies. I'd pay him the ultimate compliment that he was probably an even worse dresser than Jack Charlton. Robbo got away with just a ribbing for that but being a chain smoker hit him in the pocket. Cloughie fined him each time he caught him having a secret fag on duty, so he used to do most of his smoking away from the ground. Despite not looking a natural athlete, the young Robbo obviously had something. No less a judge than Don Revie selected him before Cloughie came for one of his England squads, obviously spotting a talent even Forest weren't totally sure of. Problem was he'd missed one thing everyone else knew – Robbo was Scottish! He'd very nearly been kicked out of Forest before Cloughie arrived in town and there were times when the gaffer himself was close to giving up on him. Robbo began to show his worth during my first season at the City Ground but was the junior wing partner for long spells. I even took the penalties!

After I'd gone, Robbo blossomed into one of the best wingers I've ever seen. He proved that you don't need pace to beat defenders, as he'd somehow do a little shimmy to throw his marker – or often markers – off balance and put over brilliant crosses. I don't think there have been many better players at smuggling their way out of a tight corner and creating chances for others. Whilst opponents often doubled up on Robbo, his control and trickery meant there was always going to be more room for others. I had one particular reason to be grateful to Robbo at Forest. After we'd played a friendly at Corby Town, he turned to me in the dressing room and said: "Now, he's someone who can play football!" That broke a lot of ice with the rest of the lads.

I'd also rate Martin O'Neill in the genuinely talented category although I'm not so sure Cloughie viewed him the same way. What I really admired about Martin was that, however many knockbacks he got from the manager, he came back and proved him wrong time after time. I was the first guy supposedly bought to replace him – although we were very different players – later it was £1m man Trevor Francis before a young Gary Mills came through the ranks. But he saw off us all to become a very important part of Forest's incredible success story. Martin wasn't as skilful as Robbo but he made up for that in sheer hard work. On a personal level, I've also got loads of time for Martin as he got over the way I was introduced to him to become a good friend. I spent happy times with him and former Radio Nottingham and Derby commentator Graeme Richards and have followed his managerial career with great interest. He may never get one of the 'top four' jobs in English football due partly to the type of football his teams play but I know he'll have been really chuffed to have landed the job at Sunderland and wish him well.

Garry Birtles is another guy I like very much but his first touch was nothing exceptional. I can't say I was that surprised when he failed to adapt to a much bigger arena at Manchester

United when he left behind the manager who transformed his career. But, boy, what a job did for Brian Clough when he needed a striker after transferring Peter Withe to Newcastle shortly after winning the First Division title. I know for sure Cloughie fancied Stephen Elliott, a fellow Forest youngster who'd been banging in the goals for the reserves and there was a feeling at the City Ground the boss was only keeping Birtles at Forest because he was a willing squash partner. But, when Elliott drew a blank, instead of getting his chequebook out he turned to someone who'd cost him £2,000 from Non League Long Eaton United and what a star he became. Yet again, Cloughie found a way of playing to Birtles' strengths as he worked tirelessly running the channels up front. The result was Garry went on to score 26 goals in a season, win two European Cup medals and represent England. That was boy's own stuff.

No one illustrated Cloughie's amazing powers of motivation better, however, than his midfielders John McGovern and Ian Bowyer. Without being disrespectful, neither were particularly great footballers. Compare and contrast them with Graeme Souness and Terry McDermott during those titanic Forest versus Liverpool clashes and it was almost embarrassing. But, again, they did what they did almost to perfection. McGovern protected the back four and was a player Cloughie could rely on week in week out to get the job done. 'Bomber' Bowyer was perhaps a more energetic and forward-thinking central midfielder but again played within his limitations and rarely let his manager down. Even Larry Lloyd, who became the rock of Forest's defence and shared a great partnership with Kenny Burns after I left the City Ground, had left Liverpool and was struggling with Coventry City when Cloughie initially took him on loan. Then there was John O'Hare, another Cloughie stalwart, who proved himself a very good all-round striker at Derby but was slightly past his best when he joined up with him again at Forest. The same could easily be applied to Frank Clark, released on a free after providing great service for Newcastle, but who became the perfect supplier to Robbo on the left hand side. Throughout that side – Woodcock, Anderson and later Francis apart – there was precious little pace but the way they kept the ball was years ahead of their time

Several of the eventual European Cup winning team were in the lineup when I made my Forest debut, along with Bryn Gunn – a substitute in the victory over Hamburg in 1980 – against neighbours Notts County on a sunny August afternoon at the City Ground. It was a touchy subject among Forest fans that, although much the bigger club, we'd been caught up by Jimmy Sirrel's side and rarely had the better of them when we came head-to-head. That afternoon was fairly typical. We had almost all of the ball and applied near constant pressure to the County goal. Yet with a very capable goalkeeper in Eric McManus between the sticks and excellent and strong defenders in Dave Needham and Brian Stubbs, the Magpies simply refused to give second best. Somehow they managed to keep the scoreline blank until the very last minute when disaster struck for us. Scottish winger Ian Scanlon looped a left wing cross into our penalty area and Les Bradd nodded home the only goal of a frustrating game at the far post.

The following weekend I was in the team as we travelled to meet Chelsea at Stamford Bridge. I had no nerves as I was just excited about the prospect of playing at such a famous ground instead of going to Bournemouth, as I would have been had I still been with Donny. The game, a boring 0-0 draw, didn't quite live up to the occasion, but I was pleased enough with my own 90 minutes. I was just glad to be in the team and learn more from Cloughie, although we weren't achieving too much. I suppose it shows how crazy it is to sack managers after a few months when one of the best managers of all took a full season and more to get Forest going. We were in the bottom half of the table most of the way through my first season at the City Ground.

For a fair while I would describe myself as being very lonely at Forest. I'd been accepted very quickly at Donny even though I'd come virtually straight off the streets into the first team but Nottingham was a different kettle of fish, I had nowhere much to go after training except my digs and travelled back home as often as I could after matches in search of company. In Nottingham my best 'mates' became the local bookies! I'd pop into William Hill after training and put £100 or so on a race. It gave me a fairly cheap thrill during otherwise quiet days and also passed the time watching the race. It was a way of coping more than anything else but threatened to get out of control, landing me in the soup with both Mum and Cloughie!

I pushed the boat out much further when for some reason I decided to draw out all the money I'd got from my cut of the transfer – nearly £4,000 – and put it on a horse. I watched the race at the betting shop and it lost! I was disappointed but not gutted which tells you a fair deal about what I'm like off-the-field. I used betting as a way of recreating some of the excitement I got from playing football. My attitude was I'd lost a lot of money but would soon go out and earn some more, so it wasn't the end of the world. Mind you, I was in trouble when I went home and Mum found the betting slip in my pocket. She phoned Cloughie to say how worried she was and he hauled me into his office for a chat. The boss enjoyed the odd bet himself and didn't tell me to quit altogether. But he did warn, if I made a habit of it, I'd never end up with much money, quoting the old line about never having seen a poor bookmaker. His message partly got through although I've always been interested in the horses throughout my life and probably contributed to bookmakers getting rich rather than the other way around. If I could give one piece of advice to young footballers now it would be to choose golf instead of betting – the other obvious way of killing time. So wags, don't nag your man when he plays golf because it could be a whole lot worse!

I got on great with Cloughie and he liked me too. Ever unpredictable, sometimes he took my breath away with his kindness. One day I reported for training as usual only to be told the gaffer wanted to have a chat with me before we started. Naturally I wondered what I had done wrong. I was completely mystified when he asked me to give him my car keys. Nevertheless I handed over the keys to my Triumph Spitfire without asking. All I could think of was that he was looking for something hidden in the car. After the session had finished, I went back nervously into his office and asked Cloughie for my keys back. He handed me a pair but when I went out into the car park I couldn't immediately spot my vehicle. "Where have you put my car, I can't see it?" I said. "Oh yes, you can – it's over there!" he said. Unbelievably, in the time I'd been training, he had sold my car and bought me a new Capri. I was flabbergasted. Cloughie had taken note of the fact I was always travelling up and down the M1 to Doncaster and wanted to ensure I had a suitable vehicle to handle all those motorway miles. "You drive more miles than James Hunt," he told me once. The way he handled the situation made me feel ten feet tall.

Another example of the Cloughie the general public didn't see came after I'd had a couple of front teeth knocked out during a game against Fulham and was feeling a bit self-conscious about going home in that state. Again the boss caught on to what I was thinking and arranged a dental appointment for me on the Sunday, taking me out for lunch afterwards with sons Nigel and Simon. As we went into the pub, Nigel made a comment about a tramp outside begging for food. Cloughie kept quiet but then sent out some Sunday lunch for the man to eat. That was the manager all over. He'd do anything for anybody, if he could, and the players themselves wanted for nothing.

I suffered a very worrying illness during my first winter at Forest which the club managed to keep from the media. On the club's advice, I had the flu jab as a precaution against the seasonal condition. I was staying in digs and woke up in the middle of the night shivering and feeling increasingly unwell.

I went downstairs and rubbed in some Ralgex. At first the club doctor thought the Ralgex could be to blame but it later became clear I'd suffered an unexpected reaction to the injection. I spent over a week in hospital as my condition got worse and worse. I shed skin, my toe and fingernails came out and I lost a fair amount of my thick curly hair. I was genuinely worried, particularly as no one was sure why this was happening. I felt so weak I didn't want to eat and my diet was limited to sipping soup for a few days. I was a very strange sight as I was red all over until my skin started to grow again – and my mop of hair returned. I was always known throughout my career for my hair which was very much in the fashion of the 70s and early 80s and almost everyone presumed was permed. But I can assure you it was 100 per cent natural.

It could hardly have been a worse start to my new career. But, thankfully, I soon started to feel better and was delighted to get myself back into the team with few people ever knowing why I'd been sidelined for a couple of months. My first Forest goal – from the penalty spot in a 4-0 win against Carlisle United at the City Ground – confirmed I was on the mend. That was a rare highlight for us during a poor first half of the season, made even worse when we were beaten 2-0 at home by West Brom on Boxing Day. I was struggling with an ankle injury and was then sidelined for another couple of months. What, I wondered, could possibly happen next?

With the side regularly firing blanks in front of goal, I recovered just in time for the return match against Chelsea at the City Ground which we lost 3-1. That was the start of a good run for me as I got myself a goal at Luton in a 1-1 draw before scoring the opener in a morale-boosting 3-0 victory over Blackpool at the City Ground. I made it three in three by netting as we won 2-0 at high-flying Bristol City and then scored with a spot kick in a seven-goal thriller a couple of weeks later when we finally saw off visitors Oldham Athletic 4-3. I saw out the season with a good run in the side as we won our last eight matches at the City Ground to finish in a more comfortable eighth position with 46 points from our 42 games. It was enough for Cloughie to award me a new two-year deal towards the end of the season when First Division strugglers Burnley first made an offer for me, then tried to take me on loan. "I'm trying to build a First Division team," said the boss. "And Curran is just the type of player I want in it."

I saw nothing of the drinking that made Cloughie such a sad figure towards the end of his 18 years at the City Ground. The squad spent a lot of time together, particularly on away trips, and his mind and body were in tip top condition. Sure, he would allow the players to relax but our alcohol consumption was under control. Sometimes he'd say 'go on have a drink' but he meant one pint rather than six or seven. I wasn't bothered anyway – I've never really been a beer drinker and would usually drink coke by the gallon. It wasn't rare for me to drink 20 or 30 glasses of the stuff and one evening I drank so much pop Cloughie actively urged me to have a glass of wine as it would do me more good. Perhaps because Cloughie was comfortable with us having a drink, there wasn't the same alcoholic culture at Forest I found at other clubs. In fact you were far more likely to see one of the lads at a concert than drinking the night away. Robbo was a huge Bryan Ferry fan. Come to think of it, he didn't look too unlike his hero either and was a pretty good singer himself. Certainly there was more chance of Robbo getting into the charts than Bryan Ferry playing on the left wing for Forest! My mate McGovern was a Status Quo man and watched his guitar heroes in action as often as possible and O'Neill, being an Irishman, was mad keen on Thin Lizzy, led by the unique Phil Lynott. Experienced full back Frank Clark didn't need to follow any musical idols, instead he used to entertain us on his guitar. Nice guy too.

Disappointing as this may be to fans of the written version of *The Damned United*, I also hardly ever heard the boss swear. There was liberal use of 'bloody' but no worse. This was the

Cloughie who put up a sign 'No swearing please, gentlemen' in front of the Trent End! We saw a good deal of Cloughie on the training ground in my first season at Forest when he took part in the five-a-sides. He insisted on us passing the ball to feet in those sessions and always complained whenever we gave him a poor pass. "Put the ball to my feet and I will score goals," he said – and he certainly did! It was easy to see why he was such a prolific striker himself before a cruel injury cut short his playing days. He then handed over a lot of that responsibility to his loyal trainer Jimmy Gordon once his assistant Peter Taylor was on the scene. The boss was at his best in the 24 hours before a game. He gave us a pep talk on the Friday, always concentrating on how good we were rather than going into great detail about our opponents. Then he'd come into the dressing room before kick off and gee us up with another great talk. Often he'd highlight the way he wanted us to play by saying airplanes were meant for the sky rather than footballs!

His tactics were very astute. His would never change something unless it was broken. Our pattern of play was as familiar as it was successful. Part of his secret was players had a natural respect for the guy. The national media talked about fear and that the guy scared us into playing out of our skins – but the opposite was more true. What he did particularly well was to help us relax and take the stress out of playing football. Often he'd give us two or three days off as he didn't want us to leave our best efforts on the training field and the boys responded as a result. Cloughie emphasised our strengths, both as individuals and as a team, and made light of our weaknesses. He never put any restrictions on the way we played and was more than happy for us to express ourselves. We went out onto the pitch convinced we could beat whoever we were playing. Cloughie was years ahead of his time as a football manager. The total priority he placed on getting the ball down and passing was a huge contrast to the more direct approach of most sides. Otherwise he placed very little emphasis on the opposition insisting they should worry about us rather than the other way round. We had a couple of free kick moves and corner routines up our sleeves but generally he encouraged us to think for ourselves on the pitch when the occasion demanded. Two of the few exceptions during my time at the City Ground were when we faced promotion rivals Bolton Wanderers, who had Sam Allardyce, Neil Whatmore and Peter Reid in their ranks, and Wolves, including the talents of John Richards and Kenny Hibbitt. If you speak to the Manchester United lads today, they'll tell you they barely consider the merits of any opponents outside the top four in the Premier Division. The truth is, whether Fergie will admit it publicly or not, other teams are scared stiff of them and half beaten before they even go out onto the pitch. I was there when Cloughie started to build the same mentality into his Forest side. When they were conquering the First Division and winning successive European Cups, he knew opponents were fearful of Forest and happy just to get players behind the ball, particularly at the City Ground. Generally, he made specific preparations only for Liverpool, the sole side during that remarkable three-year period with the ability to take on and beat Forest at their own game. To Cloughie's great credit, Forest even had the edge over the mighty Merseysiders in those clashes.

Whenever Cloughie spoke, it was obvious he knew what he was on about and had the record to prove it. He was a winner at Derby County and we knew he could be a winner again. Most of the lads towed the line with him, recognising he was in charge and picked the team. The two players most likely to challenge him were Larry Lloyd and Martin O'Neill. Lloyd made it pretty clear he didn't like Cloughie much. Lloydy always thought he was right, so was never going to back down and apologise. The dislike was mutual but, to his credit, Cloughie never let it affect his team selection. He knew Lloyd was good, so his name was always one of the first on the teamsheet. Not allowing your personal feelings to cloud your judgement is a sign of good management.

O'Neill frustrated Cloughie and he knew it. The manager was smart as a button talking about football but more than met his match in the intellectual Irishman. Martin didn't so much argue with the boss but engaged him in deep discussions, whether about the game or other subjects. They had a running verbal battle about his role in the team. O'Neill wanted to play in the centre of midfield but Cloughie almost always played him on the right hand side. There was only going to be one winner of that one. Cloughie picked the side and famously told him, if he didn't want to wear the number seven jersey, he could always swap it for a 12! On other subjects, however, Martin got the upper hand and that annoyed Clough. One of his great loves was the law and on his days off he'd often go to the courts and tell interesting tales of what he'd seen and heard. I recall him talking about the trial of serial killer Donald Neilson, known as the Black Panther, who was caught and tried locally.

What did make me cringe about Clough was the way he addressed directors. Forest were the only club run by a committee with no powerful authority figure in charge. Cloughie was lucky he could trample all over them at the City Ground. One of the guys he never seemed to get on with was Derek Pavis, who was on the committee at Forest before later going over the Trent to become chairman of Notts County. Because Cloughie didn't think they knew very much about football, he never allowed the chairman or any of the committee into the dressing room as was quite normal at other clubs. Taking a business stake in a football club doesn't guarantee someone is a football expert, but Cloughie wasn't always right. He famously bought players for Derby County without even informing the chairman Sam Longson. Not many chairmen would put up with that or accept Cloughie's point of view that they shouldn't even question the way he spent the club's money.

He was very unpredictable with journalists – absolutely charming one day, treating them like scum the next. That's if he turned up at all. One media man he clashed swords with, albeit in a playful way was Clive Tyldesley, later the voice of ITV commentary but then a young reporter with Radio Trent. We went by train to some away games and this particular Saturday we were on our way to Orient. Clive turned up at the railway station in good time only to be greeted by Cloughie a few minutes before we were due to set off. "Good morning, young man," he said in his customary drawl. "Thank you for travelling with us at Nottingham Forest but you will need a tie!" The polite reporter said he was sorry and would definitely have one in future only for Cloughie to repeat his message still more firmly. So Clive rushed off to a nearby charity shop, grabbed a tie and ran back to the station with seconds to spare. Cloughie rounded it off by saying: "Good morning young man, you are smartly dressed today!"

Lift off began when Cloughie was joined by his old sparring partner Peter Taylor. There's no doubt both men were at their best when they were together – they somehow provided more security for each other and enjoyed almost all of their success in management as a partnership. However I found their relationship strange to say the least. They argued more than an average married couple – the type who could neither live together nor be happy apart. Taylor was the insecure half of the double act and a complex character. I never got on with him at all and that played a major part in my premature exit from the City Ground. He was a gambling man – it didn't matter whether it was football, cricket or the horses – and Cloughie pulled him out of the financial mire more than once. But it was his dislike for taking responsibility that annoyed me most. The guy told us one thing when Cloughie's wasn't around and something completely different when the two were together. I never really trusted Taylor and found him rude to be honest. Several times I warned Cloughie about Taylor's backstabbing and the fact they fell out in the end didn't surprise me at all. Taylor's reputation was for spotting players although, from what I saw, he more often came up with established talents such as Shilts and Francis rather than unearthing unknown gems. Word went round the game that the dynamic duo began to fall out when this ability seemed to desert Taylor; Cloughie was none too impressed with either Justin Fashanu, for whom Forest paid out £1m to Norwich City, or fellow striker Peter Ward, from their old club Brighton. What can never be denied, however, was that during many good times, Cloughie was a happier man whilst Taylor was around. Taylor certainly made Cloughie laugh and therefore a better, more relaxed manager to deal with.

One of the ways in which Cloughie and Taylor were more on the ball than managers of their era was how much background they knew about their eventual signings – and the way they kept tabs on us. Cloughie knew all about me coming from a large family of brothers and the fact my parents split up when I was young. Coming from a big family himself gave us more in common. More mysterious was the amount of information he had about my social life. Whenever I got into a tangle at a Nottingham night spot or at the bookies it was amazing how quickly word got back to the manager and I was hauled in for a fatherly chat. In fact whether I was out and about in Doncaster or Nottingham, he was all too aware of my gallivanting with girls and the places I was going to. It's quite possible he had me followed although I know managers often received letters from fans telling them what their players were up to.

I wasn't too worried about the close scrutiny and, in some ways, took it as a compliment – he had paid good money for me and didn't want to see me waste my talent. Frequently during those first few months at Forest he warned me against spending too much time in night clubs and dating lots of different girls. "Find yourself a nice girl and settle down," he told me. Again he surprised me after I met Kim, a young woman from Kinsley, and started dating her. "You seem to be going out with one young lady more than the others," he said. "Why don't you get married?" One of Cloughie's many quirks was his insistence we should settle down and get wed. It's no secret he talked to us one-to-one and explained his views on why a settled relationship was far better than searching for night life out in the city. I'd almost call mine an arranged marriage – arranged by Brian Clough! I could see how Cloughie's view on marriage benefited the team. For some lads finding a girl and making a life-long commitment worked just great. Unfortunately I wasn't one of them.

Kim and I got married at a church in Hemsworth in May 1976 at the end of my first season with Forest. John McGovern was my best man and somehow I spent the reception watching England play Scotland in the home international. Kim was such a nice girl she didn't complain. After living in digs and then with the apprentices in a hostel at West Bridgford, I bought my first ever house – a four bedroomed property in a village close to Nottingham – and went through the motions of settling down. Problem was I never really had any intention of living the married life. Girls almost throw themselves at footballers and when a gorgeous-looking woman offers you sex when you're in a hotel room feeling lost, it takes a strong bloke to say no – and I didn't. Opportunities to stray came on our away trips. When we stayed overnight in a hotel on a Friday night, I'd start chatting to a woman and take my chance when the other lads went down for their evening meal. I'd get a message to Cloughie that I only wanted a sandwich and spend time entertaining the woman in my room. There was usually about an hour and a half to play with before my room mate returned – time enough to get to know her a whole lot better. These were good looking women happy to have sex and know they'd never see me again. I can't recall anyone causing me any grief afterwards. Cloughie hadn't a clue what I was doing. You may wonder how this was seeing as he usually knew everything about me – but sometimes people don't see what is going on under their nose! Cloughie and

Taylor constantly checked our rooms after 10pm to ensure we weren't up to anything. But by then I'd already had my fun and was only too happy to go to sleep.

There are advantages being a womaniser rather than drinking or gambling. Hiding alcohol isn't easy – you can try to mask the smell with garlic but the evidence is usually there on your breath and it will affect performance on the field; gambling will also come out into the open, too, if you are suddenly short of money and acting in a strange way; but sex was easier to keep behind closed doors – at least in those days. Today a woman can take a snap on a mobile phone and your indiscretion can become public knowledge almost instantly.

Training also showed how far Cloughie was ahead of the pack. Whereas most of my other clubs concentrated on hard, physical work, Cloughie preferred playing five-a-side and practicising in a closer, more confined environment the all-important art of keeping the football. He always simplified things but also taught us well how to handle opponents who used direct tactics. Larry Lloyd and co would drop deeper to win the ball then we'd keep it away from our opponents for as long as possible. Our short passing game was a revelation and opponents weren't used to dealing with it. Cloughie told us that, if we could keep opponents chasing the ball for 70 minutes using up priceless energy just trying to stop us scoring, we'd get our rewards in the last quarter when they got knackered. That worked better and better as the Forest success story went on.

He was also the master of another kind of football so commonplace today. Away from home, we were more cautious, dropped back and let the opposition come at us. Yet we were primed to strike at almost any moment with a lightening and very precise counter attack. He drummed into us the fact that the home team were most vulnerable pouring forward in an attempt to dominate on their own pitch and Forest gained excellent away results by hitting teams on the counter punch. It was certainly a great tactic in Europe where

Forest were almost as unbeatable on foreign soil as at the City Ground. Although his hatred for Don Revie was the stuff of legends, Cloughie did borrow at least one routine from his predecessor at Elland Road. When we were visiting London, in particular, he liked us to walk the final part of the way to the ground. Again that is something you can scarcely imagine happening in these safety-conscious days!

Training wise we did our hard work in pre-season and the first few months before leaning on Cloughie's supreme man management skills to keep us on track when the going got tough later on. His genius was in getting the best out of individuals and he did it particularly cleverly. Sometimes Robbo and I were weaving our spells on the flanks whilst John McGovern and Ian Bowyer were struggling in midfield. Cloughie took the trouble at half time to raise their spirits by insisting McGovern and Bowyer were doing all our running and were our best players. That did their morale no harm at all when he feared the fans would get on their backs before ensuring we got our portion of praise when our job was complete after the final whistle.

Cloughie was one of the first managers to see the sense of taking his players on a mid-season break – and I wasn't going to complain about that. The manager's thinking was to get away from the bad weather in England and give our bodies and minds much-needed relaxation before returning for the next game. His usual destination was Spain and one trip to Torremolinos on the Costa del Sol could easily have cost him one of our better players. Tony Woodcock, Robbo, Martin O'Neill and I decided to ignore Cloughie's warning and break the boredom by having a go on the mopeds through the woods. Woody, in particular, was completely fearless, leading us into a false sense of security. He managed to clean jump this dyke by revving up his bike to the max – no problem for him, but could the rest of us follow suit? Martin had a go and wasn't nearly so good. His bike hit the top of the dyke, the wheel got stuck and he was dragged anything up to about 100 yards. We looked on in shock wondering what was going to happen. When he finally ground to a halt, his leg was a mess but, thankfully, he wasn't too badly injured. It could so easily have been a whole lot worse. Martin nursed the injury as best as he could and we kept the truth from Cloughie

We actually began the 1976-77 season slowly although I will always remember opening day at Craven Cottage where I scored what I consider to be my best ever goal. Picking the ball up on the halfway line, I beat four defenders before lobbing the ball high into the net beyond goalkeeper Richard Teale. To make the moment still more special George Best was in the stands to see it as he was on the verge of signing for Fulham. The game finished in a 2-2 draw and Bestie said of my performance: "I was really impressed. He is a very good player." I couldn't have been more chuffed had the comments come from The Queen! To make the occasion even better I got the chance to meet my lifelong idol in the player's lounge afterwards and he personally congratulated me on my display.

We were still searching for our first win when we entertained Wolves in our third match and I suffered a rare failure from the penalty spot. This particular effort was saved as our frustration continued with a 3-1 defeat at the City Ground. After taking just three points from four games, we were 2-0 down at home to newly-promoted Hereford United before a fantastic individual goal from Ian Bowyer inspired us to a thrilling 4-3 success. That was the start of an unbelievable City Ground run as we thrashed Carlisle United 5-1 and went one better in humiliating Sheffield United 6-1, gaining some revenge over their new boss Jimmy Sirrel for all his successes over us whilst at Notts County.

The City Ground crowd was really warming to me, enjoying seeing a genuine winger who took on the full back. Often I'd flip the ball one side of my man and run around the other, sometimes going onto the cinder track by the edge of the pitch and back onto the field again. The locals begun to liken me to

Duncan McKenzie, another showman who lit up Forest a few seasons previously when they'd reached the quarter finals of the FA Cup and that infamous tie at Newcastle United when home fans invaded the pitch with Forest leading 3-1. Although our away form wasn't as good, the local press was full of it, speculating on whether we could keep the sequence going by hitting our next visitors Burnley for seven. Cloughie was full of praise for how I was playing. In one memorable article he said that, whilst Steve Coppell and Gordon Hill were tearing up trees with their wing play at Manchester United, I could have been the toast of England if I'd been at Old Trafford.

I played a part in winning the first trophy in the Forest success story – the Anglo-Scottish Cup. We started by coming through the group stages against English clubs, including Bristol City and Notts County, before our first true 'European' tie against Kilmarnock in the quarter final. This tie was played over two legs and, after beating the Scottish side 2-1 at the City Ground, we looked to be heading out at 2-0 down in the return before Robbo went on a run and set me up for a goal to take the tie into extra time. The Killies then made a bad defensive error in the first period of extra time allowing O'Hare to slip me through for what proved to be the winner. It was during my injury break that Forest went on to lift the cup with a 5-1 victory over Orient in the final again over two legs. The football world didn't take a blind bit of notice, but Cloughie was ecstatic. He was wise enough to realise that winning can be a habit and a bug of the very best kind and regarded that triumph as seriously as if we'd won the European Cup itself. It didn't matter to him whether we were playing Notts County in the County Cup, a testimonial or a crunch league game, he wanted to win – and would pick the side to do it. The game may be very physically demanding but goodness knows what Cloughie would have made of today's rotation methods with star players often sitting out of cup ties. It doesn't make a lot of sense to me either to be quite honest.

Little did I know it but Saturday, October 23 1976 and the

City Ground match against Burnley was to prove one of the turning points not only in my football career – but in life itself. I scored an early goal as we set off like an express train taking a 2-0 lead inside the opening 15 minutes but, although we eventually triumphed 5-2, this was an afternoon I remember for all the wrong reasons. John McGovern mistimed a tackle on Burnley's Paul Fletcher who accidentally caught me on my knee. I collapsed in a heap near the touchline. There wasn't any pain at first but my knee was locked and I needed to be helped off and back around the pitch into the dressing room. I was taken straight to hospital for an X-ray where it quickly became clear the injury was worse than first thought – damage to my cruciate ligament. Seeing Cloughie that night after the game on my crutches he told me the club would do everything they possibly could to help. When I hobbled out he told the local media, including the much respected Nottingham Evening Post reporter John Lawson, "promotion has just walked out of the window." Another bitter irony of that terrible day was I found out England manager Don Revie had been in the stands as he was considering selecting me for the Under 23 squad. That, as it turned out, was the closest I ever came to fulfilling my lifetime ambition of representing my country.

I needed an operation within 24 hours at Harlow Wood Hospital, the same place where I'd recovered from my infection, and was in a lot of pain. This was the injury that ended Cloughie's career and did so much damage to Paul Gascoigne. Told I'd be out for six months, I promised myself I'd be playing much sooner. I was in plaster for six long weeks and it was two months before I emerged from hospital. This was the first serious injury of my career and couldn't have come at a worse time. I was discovering my best form, the team was flying and I had every reason to be very optimistic. Then an innocuous challenge had taken all that away.

Forest lived up to Cloughie's kind words. Both the manager and the lads were absolutely brilliant in giving every possible support. They were frequent visitors, along with Kim, which I really appreciated as it was boring just sitting there with my leg in the air. I wasn't the ideal patient as I always like to be on the move. The nearest I got to football was tuning in on a Saturday to the 15-second reports on Radio Nottingham which was as much coverage as you got. I wasn't worried about winning my place back I just wanted to hear the lads were doing well. Results were mixed but generally Forest were either in or on the verge of the top three as, at long last, I found myself back on the training ground. I was feeling great but being young and fit, I thought I was much better than I actually was. Cloughie wisely told me I couldn't join in with the other lads – which I was desperate to do – until I was fit enough to do 20 laps of the City Ground pitch. I presumed the operation had been a complete success and had totally sorted out my problem. In retrospect, I may have come back too quickly although that's not a criticism of anyone. I was chomping at the bit to play my part in the business end of Forest's promotion challenge and Cloughie wanted me back as we were struggling in front of goal.

I was disappointed not to be in contention for the visit of Fulham who had Bestie, Rodney Marsh and Bobby Moore in their line up when they visited the City Ground. We won the match 3-0 and I had the great pleasure of meeting Bestie again and getting the great man's autograph. That result proved a false dawn as three successive 2-1 defeats not only saw Southampton end our hopes of FA Cup glory but left us in fifth spot, four points behind Wolves in the third and final promotion place. Cloughie and Taylor earmarked the trip to bottom of the league Hereford United on Tuesday, March 2 for my long-awaited comeback. I'd been out for just over four months, so was still well ahead of schedule but far from 100 per cent fit. Hereford gave us a close game that night but in the 38th minute came my golden moment. Robbo crossed, Bowyer had an effort blocked and I volleyed into goal at the far post. We held on to win 1-0 to gain two much-needed points and I walked off feeling pretty pleased with life. But the way I was treated afterwards by Peter Taylor took the gloss off the occasion. "You didn't put your foot in, Terry," he told me afterwards. Put my foot in! I was always a brave player, particularly so for a striker, but I'd just been maimed for months and was naturally feeling my way back a little. I didn't like his attitude and that proved another significant moment towards cutting short my Forest career.

The following Saturday saw me starting again in another tense afternoon at Carlisle. The scoreline remained blank until the last few minutes. Robbo finally put us ahead from the penalty spot only for the Cumbrians to equalise almost immediately before I set a late chance for Woody which I'm still not sure how he missed. That was actually my last meaningful contribution in a Forest shirt. An important midweek Nottingham derby followed at the City Ground with both sides still in touching distance of the top three. When my name wasn't on the team sheet I was absolutely furious and stormed into Cloughie's office to ask why. He tried to placate me but I was having none of it and slammed the door so hard on my way out it actually came off its hinges. To his credit, the great man swung round in his chair in laughter. Good job he saw the funny side of it! The joke was on me though as I was sidelined for the crucial end to the season.

It looked for most of the way as if we would just miss out but a great March and beginning of April when we produced five successive wins, including a crucial 3-1 success over close rivals Bolton Wanderers at the City Ground, put us back into third going into the run-in. It was a weird end to the season and one that could never happen nowadays. When we rounded off our campaign with a 1-0 victory over Millwall at the City Ground the home fans didn't know whether to laugh or cry. With Wolves and Chelsea already promoted, Bolton still had three games to play and needed five points out of six to overhaul us.

Cloughie wasn't going to sit and wait for the outcome. He

famously discovered his Derby County side had won the First Division title on their end-of-season holiday after Don Revie's Leeds United and Liverpool stumbled at the final hurdle. Strangely, history repeated itself. Bolton scrambled a 2-1 home victory over Cardiff City but, as they prepared to entertain champions Wolves at Burnden Park, we were flying out to sunny Spain. From our high vantage point we had no idea what was happening as Bolton needed another three points out of four to consign Forest to yet another season in Division Two. The tension was suddenly broken when the pilot made a dramatic announcement. "I'd like to congratulate Brian Clough and his Nottingham Forest players, who are on the plane today, for achieving promotion to the First Division!" We found out later that Wolves had somehow scrambled a 1-0 victory, holding on to an early goal despite having to put midfielder Willie Carr in goal for the whole of the second half. The trip certainly went with a swing after that and I was really looking forward to the challenge of playing against the best players in the country – at Liverpool, Everton, Manchester City, West Brom and Aston Villa.

I had every reason to think I was still in the manager's plans. These days a promoted side would almost certainly make wholesale changes in the summer but that wasn't the case at Forest. The sole newcomer before the 1977-78 season kicked off was Kenny Burns, a striker from Birmingham City. I say striker because I'd seen him score a fair few goals from that position but Cloughie and Taylor had earmarked a place for him in central defence alongside Larry Lloyd, as Sammy Chapman, a Trent End hero for many years, had just about run his course.

Our pre-season tour of Austria produced some morale-boosting victories but another dent in my already bad relationship with Taylor. There was a lot of attention focused on Burnsie as he was known as a bit of a lad at Birmingham. Taylor had gone out of his way to check on Burnsie and his lifestyle and assured Cloughie he would fit into our plans. We were sat outside one of the pubs which was laid out in blocks of 12 seats. Our new signing was obviously totally blasted out of his head and being sick all over the place. Taylor, who knew Kenny liked a drink, came over and asked which of us had taken him out. Robbo and Martin O'Neill were sat there and I stood up for them and said it was me. Taylor then accused me of leading Kenny astray but Cloughie was more sympathetic. "Don't take it out on Terry, he doesn't drink," the boss said. Taylor's gripe was that he'd stuck his neck on the line to sign Burnsie and was worried about getting the blame if the spirited Scotsman let us down. That was fairly typical of the guy's paranoia.

Cloughie tried to get us to sign contracts in the pre-season offering us – if that's the right word – a £25 bonus for every win in the top flight. Lloydy, being the most rebellious of the players, immediately led the revolt by saying there was no way he was going to sign it. O'Neill was also full of bluster. I was part of the revolt as well whilst John McGovern and Ian Bowyer nodded their agreement with us. Peter Taylor walked straight into the argument and, typically, said it wasn't his responsibility and Cloughie would sort us out. So in came the boss tapping away with his squash racket as if to admonish a group of naughty schoolboys. "Sign it," he waved to each of us in turn. O'Neill, who often expressed his views when Cloughie wasn't around but rarely confronted him, was one of the first to put pen to paper and all the other lads, apart from me and Lloydy did the same. It didn't matter very much as we all got the bonus anyway!

For whatever reason, I wasn't in the Forest team which kicked off at Goodison Park in sunny August. Cloughie had John Robertson on one side and O'Neill, the player I'd originally replaced, in my position on the right. We made a great start with a 3-1 win against a very strong Everton side and followed up with home victories over Bristol City and arch rivals Derby County. All was going very well for Forest, but not for me. My priority was to be in the team as I didn't want to be kicking my heels on the bench or out of the side altogether for anyone – not even the great Brian Clough. It's possible the boss was worried about whether he could play two genuine wide men in Robbo and me and instead opted for Martin, who was more a midfield player who played on the flank and offered him more insurance defensively. I put in several transfer requests and Cloughie did his best to dissuade me. He made it quite clear he liked me and that I would get my first team chance sooner rather than later. I just needed to get my head down and work hard. Great advice – I just wish I had taken it.

One particular attempt to tell Cloughie how I felt finished in complete farce. I wrote out my transfer request and went into the offices determined to find the boss. Unable to do so, I walked into Taylor's office instead with a few pieces of paper in my hand. He had his feet up on his desk and his manner annoyed me even more than usual. "I've come to see the organ grinder, not the monkey!" He told me Brian wasn't around but he could handle my problem. I was determined to make my point and quick. I slapped a piece of paper on Taylor's desk, demanded he gave it to Cloughie and stormed out.

I was in my car when I saw Taylor rushing across the car park. I was really angry as I wound the window down. Couldn't he just do that one simple thing for me?

"What the hell do you want me to do with this, Terry?" he asked.

"Just give it to Cloughie," I shouted back.

"What do you mean? It's your electricity bill!" he said. The story has done the rounds over the years with a few different names inserted but, yes, it was me. In my haste I'd given him the wrong piece of paper! You just have to laugh, don't you?

I knew Tommy Docherty was interested as one of my best mates at Forest, goalkeeper John Middleton, who had just tied up a deal with Derby, phoned to ask if I wanted to make the same switch. So I went into Cloughie's office and asked him straight whether anyone had been in for me. He called my bluff by saying I could have a new gig if I wanted – Gigg Lane, Bury, in the Fourth Division! Cloughie said they wanted me for a month, probably thinking I'd be insulted and more likely to settle down again at Forest if I thought the Shakers were my best alternative. Instead I replied by saying: "Right, so I'm off to Bury then!" The mind games continued when, after I'd played a couple of games, Cloughie rang me up at the hotel where I was staying and ordered me to tell the Bury manager I was wanted back at the City Ground straightaway. Bury boss Bobby Smith was none too impressed as he'd been offered me for a full month and phoned Cloughie whilst I was with him in his office. To my amazement, Cloughie totally backed down, insisting he'd not contacted me at all since the start of my loan spell. That hung me out to dry, making me seem like a liar and a troublemaker. Smith took it that my heart wasn't in it at the Fourth Division club and sent me back to Forest a fortnight early.

Eventually Cloughie got the message and confirmed Tommy Doc wanted me the other side of the A52. But he hadn't given up on keeping me at the City Ground. I went to see the Doc and basically made my mind up to go but Cloughie sat me down and said it didn't have to end that way. I could tear up the proposed deal with Derby and there was still a future for me at Forest even after all I'd said and done. "I was the one who wanted you here in the first place and I will put you back into the Forest team and make you into a top player," he told me. But I wanted a guarantee of first team football and that's why I was determined to go

In an ironic twist of fate almost the same moment I walked out of the door the man who did most of all to transform a promising Forest side into an almost unbeatable one was walking in. I only had the briefest of relationships with Peter Shilton, a goalkeeper who'd already shown his class between the sticks with England but who had fallen out of favour and been in a beaten Stoke City side at Mansfield just before Cloughie made his move. There were plenty who disagreed with the idea of spending £200,000-plus on a goalkeeper but that surely was the snip of the century as Shilts regained his world class form to provide Lloyd and Burns and co with the best possible insurance policy. There was an aura about the bloke at his very best. Take it from me, forwards were affected when they saw Shilts and froze. They thought they'd have to hit the perfect shot to beat him and often missed the target completely as a result. Typically Shilts, a renowned gambling man, asked whether I was interested in the horses before giving me one of his 'hot tips'. The horse finished about eighth but fortunately the guy was spot on where it really mattered for Brian Clough.

If only I could have put an older head on my young shoulders. I turned my back on one of the most successful sides of that generation – of any generation. That Forest side, with Peter Shilton in Middleton's place in goal and Archie Gemmill alongside his old sparring partner John McGovern in the middle of the park, went on a fantastic run to win the First Division title at the first attempt, finishing an amazing seven points clear of European Cup winners Liverpool. They also won the League Cup at the expense of Bob Paisley's multi-talented side and reached the quarter finals of the FA Cup. Yet that was only the start. The following two seasons saw Forest conquer Europe twice, finish runners up in the league and add another League Cup to the trophy cabinet just for good measure.

Cloughie was one of the first to see the importance of building from the back. He always said his goalkeeper was even more vital than his centre forward and that proved to be true when Shilton produced a string of brilliant displays for Forest to regain his place as England's number one. Also key in that side, of course, were Burnsie, whose pre-season fall from grace, didn't prevent him from being voted Footballer of the Year, and Lloyd, who'd been so reluctant to sign in the first place. I could and should have been a part of that. I'm convinced Cloughie would have stood by me and I would have got my place back in the side. But, as Forest set off on an adventure that took the whole of Europe by storm, I was on my way a dozen miles or so up the A52 to Derby to work for another of the most high profile managers of the time.

Talk about regrets! Nottingham Forest was a huge missed opportunity and that injury against Burnley a major turning point in my career. Had I remained injury-free that promotion season or bitten my tongue and got my head down to work my way back into the First Division team, I honestly believe I would have been involved in one of the greatest success stories in modern club football and even gone on to play for my country which is the greatest privilege of all. I had the backing and belief of a football genius in Brian Clough. He was completely unfazed by the fact I was a maverick. He'd have backed his man-management skills to get the best out of anyone including George Best!

Some people might find it strange that Cloughie and I got on so well. But our relationship hinted why Cloughie stood out from so many top managers and it really was England's loss when the FA took a conservative decision and appointed Roy Greenwood as successor to Don Revie in Forest's Championship season. A lot of players were quiet in the manager's company, perhaps feeling overwhelmed by him, but he enjoyed the cut and thrust of being with someone who had personality and talked back at him. He didn't agree with many of the things I said but he never denied me the opportunity to express my opinions, just as he never restricted me from being an individual on the pitch. That's why, unlike Revie and Greenwood, he would have had no problem handling very talented and volatile characters who remained on the fringe of the England side such as Stan Bowles and Charlie George, who both spent short spells with him at Forest. There are managers who are scared of being overshadowed by one of their players – Cloughie was the opposite. He was confident in his own skin and enjoyed being with people with talent.

My Dad, who stood by me whatever I did in life, was so angry with my decision that he threatened to wash his hands of me when I told him I was quitting Cloughie and Nottingham Forest. "You'll always regret leaving me," said Cloughie, as I walked out the door. "Everything I have done for you and you have thrown it all away . . ." How those words haunt me even to this day. If I see Cloughie in Football Heaven, I'll thank him again for the way he dealt with me and for providing me with a great philosophy of how the game should be played. The man was pure genius . . .

4

Doc, Bally and Wembley

TALK about leaving the future champions, I could so easily have been joining the top team in the country a few miles along the A52. I had no reason to think I was taking a backward step joining a side including fantastic players such as Charlie George, Gerry Daly, Roy McFarland, Colin Todd, David Nish, Bruce Rioch and Don Masson and with Gordon Hill soon to follow. Blimey, they'd won the First Division for the second time just three years before under Cloughie's successor Dave Mackay and enjoyed their fair share of success in Europe as well.

After Cloughie at Forest, moving to Derby County meant playing for another of the game's most high profile managers in Tommy Docherty. But that's where the similarity ended. For while Cloughie fully lived up to all the good things I'd heard about him, this wasn't the best time to bump into The Doc. To be fair, his appointment at the Baseball Ground came at a low point of his managerial career. His dream job at Manchester United had blown up in his face due to problems in his private life. That's an unusually polite way of saying he'd 'been up Mary Brown', the wife of the club's physiotherapist! United ensured he finished on a playing high when they beat Liverpool 2-1 in the 1977 FA Cup final at Wembley but not even a few Hail Marys could prevent The Doc from getting the sack. Although he'd managed at smaller clubs earlier in his career, I don't think Tommy adjusted to the culture shock of coming back into the real world at Derby after being a constant source of national attention at Old Trafford. Let's face it, clubs don't come any bigger than Manchester

United and it can't be easy for any player or manager to leave, particularly in the way he did. I saw no shortage of The Doc's familiar wise cracking at Derby – but, in my view, his heart was still at Old Trafford.

Doc must have been looking the other way at times during my six months at the Baseball Ground as the drinking and cards culture took the players' minds off the small matter of the football. When he found out what was going on under his nose, it was all too late. He tried to tackle the problem by clearing out the troublemakers but the horse had long since bolted. We only showed flashes of what we were capable of as we finished mid-table. League champions Liverpool, including Graeme Souness and Kenny Dalglish, were put to the sword one March evening when we beat them 4-2 and looked more like title winners ourselves. There were few places to match the old Baseball Ground and not just because the fans were very close to the pitch. Rams supporters are some of the most passionate in the country and the atmosphere on floodlit evenings such as that was something else. But all too often we played a long way short of our potential.

The Derby experience taught me a very valuable lesson: no matter how good a team is you haven't got a prayer unless the dressing room is right. Had the Doc got that team to play together and organised us as a unit we could easily have stolen Forest's thunder. Man for man I don't think many would dispute we were better than them – but, as a team, we weren't in the same league. I'm convinced the other difference between mediocrity and challenging for another title was down to the position Cloughie convinced me was the most important on the football field. I was a friend of John Middleton and rated him as a good goalkeeper but one prone to mistakes. Yet, if we'd had Peter Shilton between the sticks, we would have gone places. Everyone talks about the value of a 20-goal a season striker but someone who can save you 12 to 15 goals at the other end is even more important in my opinion.

Not seeing too much of The Doc on the training ground didn't really matter as we had a good coach in Frank Bluntstone. But even in those last few minutes before we went out to play, there wasn't any real evidence of motivation or tactics. Doc would just be his normal self, cracking jokes and generally taking the mickey, but I don't think the lads ever really trusted the guy. What I did like was that his team was committed to attacking football. He picked wingers and stuck with the 4-4-2 formation he used at United with me on one flank and Gordon Hill on the other. If it worked, all was well – if it didn't, he'd get different players. Like Harry Redknapp today, The Doc was a constant chopper and changer which didn't really make for a settled line up. He used no fewer than 31 players in that hectic season. Some Derby lads regarded The Doc as a compulsive liar; porkies flowed so naturally from his lips he almost believed them himself, they said. That was harsh. Managers often tell a player what he wants to hear, whether truthful or not. Telling players who aren't in the side exactly what you think would soon lead to a procession to the exit door!

I didn't play as consistently well as I know I could have at the Baseball Ground even though I was one of the few regulars. Like when I was a teenager and wrote a letter to the Doc congratulating him on his appointment at Old Trafford in 1973, I was a little in awe of the talent around me. From my spot wide on the right, I spent too much time admiring the skills of Charlie George, probably the most talented guy I ever played with, and too little imposing myself on the game. Just watching Charlie in training was an education in itself and he happened to be one of the nicest guys you could possibly meet who'd do anything for anybody off the field. Charlie was very, very special; a true crowd pleaser, he had that rare ability to make good opponents look like mugs. It was almost a criminal waste he only played 60 odd minutes of one international for Don Revie's England – and that out of position on the wing. I admired Revie greatly for his achievements at Elland

Road but, as England boss, he must take responsibility for ignoring some of the most talented players this country has ever produced such as Frank Worthington, Tony Currie and Stan Bowles. All were unpredictable and had their faults but, if you are ever going to beat the best teams in the world, you need players with real ability. The sad truth was Revie and England couldn't handle them.

It all started well enough as I made my Rams debut in a 2-1 home victory over West Ham United in November, a victory that kick started a good run of form. My eyes were opened later in the month to what the Doc was missing when we travelled to Ashton Gate to face Bristol City. The card school, including Gerry Ryan, Gerry Daly, Charlie George, Roy McFarland and yours truly, soon had between £600 and £700 in the pot. We were playing three card brag and the heat was too much for Toddy who decided to quit. I should have done the same as, by the time the game had finished, I was £800 down. Like the loss on the horses at Forest that didn't worry me too much. I've never let things like that get to me. But I can imagine the damage players owing big sums of money to colleagues had on the morale of the team as a whole. Players started games having lost the equivalent of a fortnight's wages. Not surprisingly, perhaps, we lost 3-1 to Bristol.

We had a Christmas 'special' before the Ipswich Town game. Checking into the hotel, the lads were looking to kill some time on the Friday night, so it was no surprise when the card game began in earnest. It wasn't just the cards that were flowing as we had two cases of wine and a huge amount of beer for company. I was there with Charlie George, Toddy, Billy Hughes and Gerry Daly, who saw red when we threw his clothes out of the window. There was a cool £1,600 in the pot and the game dragged on and on until about 4am – remembering we were due to get up a few hours later to begin our pre-match preparations! You probably think we took a festive tonking from Bobby Robson's side. Wrong! Somehow we went home with an unlikely 2-1 victory after my mate

Charlie came up trumps with one of the best goals I've ever seen. That was typical of the bloke.

January 1978 produced an occasion I'd always looked forward to – my first senior game at Old Trafford – but it ended in disappointment as we were whipped 4-0 by a rampant United. Match of the Day cameras captured my first ever goal in the top flight but it wasn't enough to prevent visitors Birmingham City beating us 3-1. We then managed to round off the season – and my Derby career – with a pair of convincing Baseball Ground victories. Local rivals Leicester City, relegated that season, were seen off 4-1 and we sent our fans into the summer break with a 3-0 success over Arsenal to complete a double over the fifth-placed Gunners. That was my 26th and final game for Derby and I ended on a high with my second goal.

My Derby career came to a crunch at the end of the season when a reporter phoned to tell me newly promoted Southampton were interested. Doc's attitude when he spoke with me made up my mind: "If you want to go, go; if you want to stay, stay," he said. When someone goes out of their way to tell you about an offer from another club, I always think it's better to move on. So I was on my way to locking swords with the third in a growing list of managers with a huge reputation and public profile – Lawrie McMenemy. He had taken the unfashionable Saints to an FA Cup Final in 1976, then overseen one of the Wembley shocks of all time as his Second Division side beat mighty Manchester United with a single goal from Bobby Stokes. But, more than that, his regular media appearances meant he was seen as a genial giant, a manager with a comparatively small club who traded punches with the best in the land and did so with a likeable charm. Everyone seemed to like him – but then most didn't have to work with him! Put it this way, I saw little evidence of any managerial magic during my season at The Dell.

Where I will give him credit was in bringing in top class experienced players such as Alan Ball, Peter Osgood, Chris

Nicholl, Ted MacDougall and Phil Boyer. Whilst I was at The Dell he brought in Charlie George from Derby and later added another very significant name to the list in England skipper Kevin Keegan. But he relied on them for more than their undoubted talent on the pitch. In my view, he surrounded himself with big names to hide his own weaknesses and, in the case of my mate Bally, almost handed over the managerial reigns. Looking at the results he achieved over the years that policy worked well and helped promote him to such status he was being talked about as a future manager of England. That would have been a complete disaster. McMenemy was always likely to be found out on a bigger stage, as when I was unfortunate enough to catch up with him again at Sunderland.

I'll always remember the first time I set eyes on Bally, a meeting that set the tone for the happier days I enjoyed on the south coast. I walked into the dressing room wearing a short leather Christian Dior jacket I'd paid a cool £400 for and light blue jeans.

Bally shouted out: "Where's your motorbike?"

"It's outside," I replied.

The banter had started straightaway. We got chatting and, like a lot of players, the great man wanted to know what it was like playing for Cloughie and said he doubted he could have coped with someone barking his orders. "He wasn't like that at all," I said. "He liked players to express themselves – you would have loved it." I'm still sure he would. As with Cloughie, you may wonder what Bally and I had in common. He was a virtual national treasure and I was a volatile young man who'd already gone through a couple of First Division clubs. On the other hand, we were both northerners. Ok, he was from Lancashire and I was from Yorkshire, but there was common ground there. Secondly, we both liked a bet. Bally was keen on the horses and did as much as anyone to increase my interest in the sport as he took me to nearby race meetings at Fontwell Park, Newbury and Sandown. Most important of all, we both loved a good night out, especially if it took up a good amount of the next day as well! There were a lot of married men in the Saints side and Bally and I were the two who nevertheless had a ticket out on the town whenever we needed one. I'll give the great man the credit for being one of the few people to get me to drink. His favourite tipple was gin and orange and he couldn't work out why I was so obsessed with coke. I told him I had a sweet tooth – I even had three sugars in my tea – and he introduced me to a wine called Piesporter that hit the spot. I hadn't been drunk since I was 18 but admit to being the worse for wear going out with Bally on a few occasions, notably a mid-season trip to Marbella when he made a few excuses for me when I was too hammered to take part in a golf match.

Bally was big in every sense apart from his short stature. I only saw him towards the end of his distinguished playing career but, judging by how good he was at Saints when his legs were going, he must have been some footballer in his prime. If ever there was an England player who could have fitted into today's brilliant Barcelona and Spain sides, it was Bally. For he played the same brand of one and two touch football with which they are dominating today. The guy was years ahead of his time. Off the field he was a real character and seemed to like fellow players with a touch of personality. My Saints life was all the better for being mates with Bally although our closeness didn't escape the notice of the green-eyed monster McMenemy who didn't take too kindly to our friendship.

One negative of McMenemy's over-reliance on the experienced lads was that cliques were formed in the dressing room with the younger players suffering as a result. One good example was Graham Baker, still a relative youngster even though he was in his second spell at Saints after rejoining us from Manchester City. I remember the lad being in tears at training because he'd been left out of the team after seemingly doing a good job and getting no explanation at all from the manager. It didn't matter whether Bally or Osgood played badly in the previous game, their influence on the boss meant their names were on the teamsheet. Suitably stirred, I took up Baker's case and confronted McMenemy. "What's it got to do with you?" he replied angrily. "I'm the manager."

"Oh, no, you're not," I snapped. "Alan Ball is!"

I was being honest. Whilst I was a Saint, the guy who picked the team was Bally, England's 1966 World Cup hero – of that I have no doubt.

It was a good job we had Bally directing the ship because McMenemy was never likely to win our respect on the training ground. One of his favourite routines was the shooting practice in which the boss was supposed to cushion the ball off for each of us to have a crack. In all honesty we spent most of those 45 minutes retrieving the ball from all areas of the training ground rather than taking shots because the bloke had the touch of an elephant. A former member of the Coldstream Guards, he played no higher himself than Non League Gateshead and you could tell. It's always tougher to take criticism from a bloke who never played at a high level himself, although ironically some of the great managers including Arsene Wenger and Jose Mourinho fall into that category. I'd also add that the best McMenemy speeches were always reserved for the media. He wasn't nearly as good with his words when it came to the important task of motivating us in the dressing room.

Imagine you were with us a few minutes before going out to play a big game against a team with potential match winners like Francis, Currie or Worthington in the opposition line up. McMenemy wouldn't focus so much on how to contain them but how to put them out of the game with as little cost to our side as possible. So, for example, he'd turn to Stevie Williams and tell him to go out and kick Currie; then it would be the turn of Nick Holmes, a fellow midfielder who never took any prisoners; the third part of the trick was usually defender Manny Andruszewski, our resident hard man. He was the guy McMenemy reserved for 'man marking' jobs, if you get what I mean.

Early on at Saints I had a niggling pain in my right leg just below the knee that gradually got worse and worse. I didn't link it in my mind with my injury at Forest, after all that had been in a slightly different place and I presumed it had been cured by the operation. It was then I was introduced to the cortisone injection and told that, if I had the jab, I'd be pain free for six months with no further complications. Seemed like a good deal to me. All I wanted was to be rid of the pain and play football and this treatment was promising just that. I have no reason to believe anyone knew any different. Saints' motives were to help their new signing get himself onto the pitch in any way they could. Once the injection settled down, it did the trick. The pain was gone and wasn't an issue for the rest of my time on the south coast.

We had a good team with the reliable Terry Gennoe between the sticks, Yugoslavian Ivan Golac at full back, burly Chris Nicholl at centre half, skilful Steve Williams complementing Bally in midfield and Phil Boyer up front. War horse Ted MacDougall was Boyer's partner during the early months of the season until he moved to Bournemouth after which McMenemy pulled off a real coup by persuading Charlie George to become his record £315,000 signing from Derby despite much interest from Cloughie. We were never good or consistent enough to challenge for honours in the First Division but always worth putting a few quid on in the cups. Bally certainly thought so as at the start of the season he put £25 each on us to win the League Cup and the FA Cup. For a long time in that memorable campaign the little man looked as if he had backed a winner.

John Bond's Norwich City provided the opposition for my Saints debut at Carrow Road where we lost 3-1 on the opening day of the First Division season. I was then substituted on my first appearance at The Dell where a typically brilliant Frank Worthington free kick enabled visitors Bolton Wanders to escape with a 2-2 draw. My show was truly on the road with a really good performance in our first victory of the campaign over Middlesbrough. Bally was ecstatic, too, after chipping a wonder goal as we gave our home fans something to shout about with a 2-1 success. McMenemy then gave hardman Manny Andruszewski one of his special missions to combat in-form Trevor Francis at Birmingham in the League Cup but the damage was done at the other end by MacDougall and Boyer with two goals each as we triumphed 5-2.

There were a couple of early reunions with the Doc as we got beaten 2-1 in the league at the Baseball Ground before a Phil Boyer goal saw them off in the League Cup at The Dell. We were largely in the bottom third of the table in the early months although we took encouragement from good performances in holding champions Forest to a 0-0 draw at home before a Nick Holmes equaliser earned us a useful point at Manchester United a week later. But it was in the League Cup where we were beginning to make progress – to Bally's delight – as we beat Reading 2-0 after a replay to get through to the last eight and a sniff of Wembley.

I'd looked forward to coming back to Yorkshire for the league match at Leeds where I had plenty of support from family and friends – but the day blew up in my face. Apparently my John Travolta-style outfit didn't get me off to the best of starts with McMenemy, particularly as I was only on the bench. There was no doubt, however, who was the flashest guy at Elland Road as Tony Currie dominated the midfield with a mesmerising personal display including a viciously bending 30-yarder past Gennoe. What did annoy us, though, was that Leeds were beginning to take the mickey, almost like in that famous 7-0 win over Saints a few seasons before when they knocked the ball around among themselves as if the visitors didn't exist. So when I eventually got onto the pitch, I decided it was my turn. I got the ball near the corner flag and, with full back Frankie Gray backing off, put my knee on the ball for my own piece of showboating. McMenemy was absolutely furious afterwards, saying he wouldn't have minded me doing that had we been 4-0 up but not when we were 4-0 down! The manager reportedly wanted me out of the club by Christmas but he hadn't seen the last of me just yet.

A mid-season break in Marbella provided some timely team bonding with Bally, in particular, making sure his glass was always full before we all showed McMenemy we could play by pulling off a notable double over Manchester City. Boyer got a goal in both games as we followed up our first away win in the league with another 2-1 success back at The Dell in the League Cup. We were now in the semi finals – just a two-legged tie away from the Twin Towers – and awaited the draw with great interest. We were happy enough to avoid Forest, who were paired with Graham Taylor's giantkillers Watford, but knew we'd have to be on great form to get past Leeds United.

Having got beaten 4-0 a few weeks earlier the first leg at Elland Road could easily have been six or seven. Currie was at his tricks again giving Leeds the lead after 25 minutes and, when Ray Hankin lashed in a second shortly after half time, our fans must have feared the worst. Football, though, can be a crazy game and this was one night when the gods were definitely on our side. From virtually our only two on target efforts we pulled the scoreline back to a very creditable 2-2 – and I was involved in both goals. First, Gennoe found me on the right flank with a long kick and my deep cross was headed in at the far post by Nick Holmes. Then I put over another centre and Steve Williams met it as sweet as a nut on the volley for the best goal of the tie after 62 minutes. Even Currie's mickey taking that led to Boyer being sent off nine minutes from time couldn't take the edge off our joy. Leeds came off the pitch deflated whilst for Bally and I a draw out of nowhere was a great result and even better excuse for a party.

We went to a night club in the city centre where I soon found myself in interesting company as Sheffield Wednesday manager Jack Charlton and his assistant Maurice Setters, my first manager at Donny, were among the party-goers.

Bally and Jack were as thick as thieves, being great mates from the World Cup team. But I was in for a surprise when Jack pointedly grabbed a word in my ear and said: "How would you like to come and play for us next season?" I was interested from the start even though it probably wouldn't have made sense to anyone else. Here I was with my third First Division club within a couple of seasons and possibly on the verge of getting to Wembley and in walks Big Jack, a bloke I didn't like too much from what I'd seen of him on TV, wanting me to drop down two divisions to play for him. The obvious answer was no, but there was one big thing in Jack's favour. As a kid, there had been two teams in my life – Sheffield Wednesday and Manchester United. As I hadn't yet had a phone call from Old Trafford, this was my dream offer. Not being close to McMenemy, I kept Wednesday's unofficial approach to myself although Bally, being a mate and within a couple of yards of me when it happened, knew all about it. So he spent the next few weeks telling me to kick Wednesday into touch and stay with him at Saints.

I hadn't heard the last of Elland Road however as I got hauled into the manager's office to explain another bizarre incident. An egg had been thrown onto the pitch – I think it was meant for Bally – and I instinctively picked it up and hurled it back into the crowd. Whilst McMenemy was none too amused, Bally's approach was more light hearted. He doubted that the egg could have remained intact and set up a challenge during which he threw six eggs at me to see if they broke. The daft bugger ensured they were hard boiled first.

We had to be up early as we were due to travel to Blackpool for an FA Cup tie at the weekend at Preston North End. That was one time I was quite happy the weather took a turn for the worse. Snow swept in and it became obvious the tie at the weekend would be in doubt. Bally's thinking was clear: game off, good night on! Bally used to compare being cooped up in a hotel with fellow footballers on a Friday night to being in prison. He got the idea from visiting a prison at Preston during his Everton days as part of the club's community work. I thought better of it on this occasion as I was in enough trouble with McMenemy already, but that didn't stop Bally. The midfield dynamo shinned his way down the drainpipe towards the bright lights of Blackpool. It was breakfast time by a conservative estimate when he performed his next piece of acrobatics to climb back into his hotel room clearly much the worse for wear. He'd been to boxer Brian London's club and obviously had a good time. Credit Bally, though, for the cup tie was postponed and no harm was done!

Despite secret doubts over my future, the second leg was a very memorable night for me for more than one reason! Like the Baseball Ground, The Dell was an intimate ground simply made for nights such as this one. The weather was perfect for football, the pitch in good condition and home fans right behind us for what we all thought was going to be a very tough challenge. Leeds were still one of the best sides in the First Division with the Gray brothers, Eddie and Frankie, Arthur Graham and, of course, Currie among their ranks. But there was no doubt who were the better team that evening as we reversed the tide of the first leg. It couldn't have gone too much better for me as I scored my first and only goal for Saints to book our place in the final. It was a good move involving Bally, Nick Holmes and Trevor Hebberd before the latter's cross just eluded Leeds full back Frankie Gray. My first shot was blocked by a defender but it rebounded to me and I lifted the ball high beyond the reach of Scottish goalkeeper David Harvey from close range. What a goal! What a moment! What a victory! All I could think of at the final whistle was that the Kinsley kid was on his way to Wembley . . .

If the match had been unforgettable, the night out that followed was just as good. Bally and I started quietly enough by going out to an Italian restaurant for a meal before things began to hot up as I took the celebrations a stage further by moving on to a club. On a high and up for anything after our victory, a mate and I soon netted ourselves a rare one-two – a mother and daughter! Things were still looking promising a few drinks later as my friend's bird – the mother, of course – invited us back to her bungalow with the assurance her husband was away. This was the perfect end to a great night with two very good looking women. What could go wrong? We were in separate bedrooms with our partners and, after a while, decided to change ends! This was the type of two legged tie I liked.

But what was that noise I could hear at the height of our passion? Shit, it was a car pulling up near the garage. That could only mean one thing – husband alert! Grabbing whatever I could, I ran into the other bedroom where my friend was still 'entertaining'. Next thing, he went flying out of the window, having just about pulled on his trousers and with his shoes in his hand. He dived over me into the back garden and straight into a huge puddle. Both of us then jumped over next door's fence and fled down the street in our dishevelled states. I still didn't have anything on my feet. Somehow we got away with it with no trace of an irate husband on our tail. We flagged down a taxi whose driver recognised me straightaway and asked him to take us home. I told him I'd been out to celebrate our victory but left out the highlights.

Of all the teams to face us at Wembley in the League Cup final it just had to be Forest. After winning the competition the previous season through Robbo's penalty against Liverpool, Cloughie's boys fought their way through to a second successive final by seeing off Watford 3-1 on aggregate. The national press were in no doubt. Forest were the First Division champions, cup holders and on their way to winning the European Cup for the first time and only had to turn up to beat Saints. The two teams prepared in very different ways. We got our heads down early in our hotel and went to sleep – yes, honestly, even Bally and me! We knew it was going to be a huge game next day and wanted to give ourselves a chance. Bright lights, women and song could wait for one night. Forest did the exact opposite. Loads has been written about how Cloughie 'relaxed' his team for that final – and, knowing the lads as I do, I can tell you it was all true.

Cloughie had some of his lads in the bar, having a jar or three or four. Then, for some reason, he told them to knock up those who'd already turned in such as Archie Gemmill and Tony Woodcock to ensure they got their fair share! They had to carry Woody back to his room when they finished. Fantastic. Meanwhile Bally had lined up our own pre-match entertainment, his mate Freddie Starr. The zany comedian was on the team coach as we left for Wembley, much to McMenemy's surprise. Then when we walked out onto the pitch prior to kick off, Freddie marched in front of the band, waving his arms around manically. McMenemy walked with me, more concerned with keeping me away from Cloughie: "This is your chance to show Forest what you can do!" he said. He probably thought it was a great piece of motivation – he needn't have bothered as I never really needed motivating for a football match.

Don't know about being relaxed, Forest looked half asleep in the first 45 minutes which wasn't surprising as they'd been on the piss all night. We were on top of our game and gave them a battering until half time. Bally produced a brilliant pass for our left back David Peach to take the ball around Peter Shilton and give us a 1-0 lead in the 17th minute, the very least we deserved. I was in opposition to Frank Clark, the experienced Geordie left back who was virtually on his last legs – through age, not beer! He wasn't going to live with me for pace, was he? Knowing Cloughie as I did, however, I knew this tie was far from over. I would have put money on him to have Forest charged up to have a real go at us after the break. Unfortunately for us, we became our own worst enemies. Nick Holmes gave the ball away to Robbo and then a misunderstanding between Chris Nicholl and the normally dependable Terry Gennoe allowed Garry Birtles to nip in for the equaliser. Birtles then outpaced Nicholl to shoot Forest into a 2-1 lead. The goals understandably increased Forest's confidence and they started to dominate before Archie Gemmill slipped Tony Woodcock through for what looked like a decisive third. Still we could have got something from the match, however, as first Nick Holmes hauled the deficit back to 3-2, and then that man Shilton made a crucial match-winning save at the death. So near and yet so far. I had a reasonable game against Frank Clark, yet we hadn't quite been good enough to stop Clough and lift the cup.

There was plenty of scope, however, for a party and Bally was in no mood to let the occasion pass by without a proper celebration. First thing he did was produce his cup final tankard with a bit of Wembley turf in it. Bless him, he'd graced the hallowed turf on countless occasions, so handed it to me to keep as I had no reason to know whether I'd ever play there again. I eventually buried that prized turf in my garden near Barnsley when I returned to live in Yorkshire. I don't know what happened to it when I left which is sad as I never did return to Wembley. Bally decided we needed to go to Tramps, one of London's top night clubs, and what a night it was. To be honest, the venue itself didn't quite live up to its glamorous reputation. but that didn't matter as the stars were out in force. Michael Caine, Oliver Tobias and Joan Collins took centre stage for some but for Les Sealey, the Luton and Manchester United goalkeeper, Queen of the Ball was definitely the gorgeous Olivia Newton John, whom he asked for a dance. But then the real star walked in. It was fantastic to see the great George Best in the flesh again and you just had to be there to believe it. All those famous folk were in the room yet the moment Bestie made his entrance all eyes – mine included – were glued to him. The guy's pulling power was truly remarkable; he was unofficially the fifth Beatle.

Looking back, I can easily see how Bestie's life unfolded. He wasn't so much a footballer as a celebrity – a magnetic personality everyone wanted a piece of. It made and ultimately destroyed him. I lived to excess at times but you can't party every night, drink and shag women and be bright and bushy tailed for training at 10am the following morning. Believe me, if it was more of us would have tried it. He may not have had a particularly long playing career or a long enough life for that matter, but the guy left so many fantastic memories. The great man is still the screen saver on my laptop so I think about him most days.

Unfortunately, the party had to come to an end because scarcely 48 hours and a lot of champagne after losing to Forest we were back at The Dell for a quarter final FA Cup tie against Arsenal. We were still full of optimism having beaten the Gunners 2-0 on our patch just a couple of weeks before and with Bally's bet still riding on the result. For much of the night we looked well capable of easing the Forest hangover as we were a goal to the good and playing well. But ten minutes from time we conceded a heartbreaking equaliser. Gennoe turned an effort onto the bar and somehow it rolled down the woodwork at the far post and perfectly into the path of David Price whose tap in denied us another semi final place. Instead we had to go to Highbury just two nights later for a replay. Did the FA have it in for us or what?

I had an interesting time that night, without getting onto the pitch. I was rooming with striker Phil Boyer when I got a phone call from Bally asking me to come to his room. He introduced me to Alan Hinton, the former Derby and Forest winger and now manager of American side Seattle Sounders. Hinton was keen to take me to the States and offered me a deal that would have given me a £12,000 signing on fee yet put a cool £17,000 in McMenemy's pocket. There was no way whatsoever I was going to be party to a deal that gave him that kind of cash for absolutely nothing. Bally advised me I was too young to sell out to America and I told Hinton politely no thanks. Bally also told me McMenemy had left me out of the side for the replay – with Charlie George, of all people, taking my place on the left wing – but not to go ballistic because similar things had happened to everyone. It was probably the last straw as far as I was concerned, though, making the move to Wednesday even more attractive. Unsurprisingly, perhaps, we lost the replay 2-0, marking the end of Bally's dream and our search for silverware. It was also, to all intents and purposes, the end for me at The Dell.

There were still a fair few First Division games to complete the season and I got myself back into the side as Bally had hinted the following Saturday for our 2-0 defeat at Bolton Wanderers. Time was against me as there were now just four days to go until the transfer deadline and I was determined to get my move to Sheffield Wednesday.

I got in touch with McMenemy whilst I was at the races the day before the deadline and really laid into him. He tried every angle in the book. First, he brought up the option of me going to America, then changed tack and offered me a three-year deal instead. I was only halfway through my initial two-year contract, so it was a good offer but my mind was firmly made up – I was going to join Wednesday. I told him he was a poor manager and I didn't want to work with him a day longer. He was still reluctant to let me go but the final straw was when I threatened to give the press a story about how he ordered us to stop talented opponents by injuring them or getting them sent off. McMenemy wasn't happy and Saints did their best to thwart the move on transfer deadline day in March. The cut off point was 5pm and I was in a car with the Saints secretary, worried because we were struggling through the London traffic to get the transfer forms to FA headquarters. Finally, I ordered a taxi and got there with five minutes or so to spare. I was coming 'home' to Yorkshire and the chance to play for another of the so-called managerial giants – Jack Charlton. Although money wasn't an issue in the move, Kim and I made a tidy £10,000 profit from selling our new house in Eastleigh to return north after just a few months.

Although I left The Dell behind so quickly, I remained good mates with Bally for many years afterwards. We had some great times together – occasions I will never forget. After one memorable night out, we got back to Bally's place at about 5am – his wife Lesley not being too impressed – and he went to the trouble of showing me his England caps and his World Cup medal. After hanging up his boots, he went into management but, like many of the very best players, was unable to repeat his success off the field. I remember catching up with him at Blackpool when he told me how frustrated he was at how his team was playing. Like Bobby Charlton when he took on Preston and years later when Arsenal and England defender Tony Adams managed at Wycombe Wanderers, Bally found it difficult to adjust to dealing with players who had nothing like his own ability. He played at the highest level throughout his career and never had any connection with the lower divisions. Bally often rang up and invited me to go to Ascot, one of his favourite weeks of the year. I last saw him about four years before his sad death in April 2007. I was driving when I heard the news on the radio that Bally had been taken ill in his garden and had passed away. There have been a couple of unforgettable times in my life when a footballer's death has brought a tear to my eye and his was one of them.

Rest in peace, Bally, you were a true mate as well as a legend . . .

5

Boxing Day Massacre and Romping to Promotion

"Terry Curran was a Sheffield Wednesday superstar – there was no one to touch him; he was the George Best of the Third Division. We still get together for Boxing Day massacre reunions – Wednesday have had great days in the First Division, in the Cups and played in Europe but that's the match the fans still talk about. Tony Kenworthy was one of the best defenders in the league but he didn't know what day it was. I scored the first goal, but Terry Curran was the player they just couldn't handle either then or at Bramall Lane. Terry was very confident and always thought he knew it all – which he didn't. We used to say 'Terry Curran is always right and Jack Charlton is never wrong'. Nothing Terry did on a football pitch surprised me but signing for Sheffield United was absolutely crazy."

Ian Mellor, Sheffield Wednesday 1979-1982

ANY AGENT would have had me shot at the very thought of dropping down two divisions at the very height of my powers. I'd done enough to be mentioned as a possible England player, so career-wise to take two steps backwards made no logical sense. But I will always be a Sheffield Wednesday fan and made the decision because it was the Owls who were asking. I had fantastic times at Hillsborough – some of my very best in football – and was thrilled to play a part in turning my club's fortunes around even if we fell just short of getting back into the First Division.

So in what sort of state did I find the club? Wednesday had

been under-performing for years. I'd always looked out for Wednesday's results whilst with my first four professional clubs and it hadn't made for very good listening. The Owls had been relegated into the Third Division in 1974-75 and 12 months later escaped going down still further by just a single point. Yet now they had a big-name manager in Jack Charlton the only way, surely, was up. In many ways I was moving to a better club as Wednesday, with an historic ground brought back up to speed for the 1966 World Cup and fantastic support, had a lot more potential than Saints. It also said something about Wednesday that they were able and willing to match my £300 a week wages I'd enjoyed at First Division Saints.

This was Wednesday's fourth season in the third flight and it was obvious we weren't going to get promoted this time either. Just about the only encouragement for Owls fans during yet another disappointing campaign had been an FA Cup third round epic against First Division giants Arsenal. Like a lot of the country, I followed the story step by step as we drew at Hillsborough in front of more than 33,000 before going down to Highbury and again finishing level. There were then three further replays, all played on neutral territory at Leicester City's Filbert Street, before the Gunners finally triumphed 2-0. Remember those golden days of the FA Cup?

I didn't really think about it at the time but here I was playing for my fourth top boss: Jack was a national hero, centre half in England's 1966 World Cup winning side and brother of the legendary Bobby. He'd come to Wednesday after a successful spell at Middlesbrough and I, like everyone else, was excited to find out what he could do. The fans remember Big Jack with a fair deal of affection – and quite rightly. He stopped the Wednesday slump as he got us back into the old Second Division and took us to the very verge of the top flight two seasons later. Yet he was far from perfect. We had plenty of ups and downs during my three years at Hillsborough – some Big Jack should take responsibility for and others when I totally lost the plot – but they were days I mostly treasure and I'll always thank the manager for that.

Players sometimes judge managers by odd things and Jack's lack of finesse on the training ground didn't win him too many Brownie points with us. But I was more concerned about his tactics. Jack was the ultimate route one merchant; he would have been the ideal manager of the old Crazy Gang at Wimbledon. As a defender, he was obsessed with keeping things tight at the back and reckoned the quicker you could hit the front men the more chance you'd have of doing damage at the other end. To be fair, he was a man of the times. Most teams played that way in the late 70s and early 80s and Jack went on to gain a fair deal of success as manager of the Republic of Ireland, taking them to the World Cup quarter final in the USA in 1994. They, too, were viewed as a horrible team to play against – not a lot of skill, but ultra competitive and difficult to beat. Little wonder Liam Brady, the Arsenal and Sampdoria star, chose Jack's appointment to opt out of international football. A midfielder with silky skills was never likely to be one of Jack's favourites.

The manager's tactics weren't ideal for me, whether playing on the right or as an unorthodox striker. He told our goalkeeper Bob Bolder to throw the ball out to Ray Blackhall our right back and urged me to drop off 10 yards as he booted it 30 yards up the line in the general direction of Andy McCulloch. The idea was for me to make up the ground to support him, but he'd have been better off putting his greyhound in the side. Later he played me up front alongside McCulloch. I thought this was my best position but playing there for Jack's Wednesday was never going to be easy. You can have all the skill in the world but when the ball's flying yards over your head there's not a striker in the world who can control it. Jack told me I was a good player with the ball at my feet but not so good with my back towards goal. "Do you know a footballer who is, Jack?" I replied. It's always better to be side-on facing the opposition's goal, the way coaches insist today. Jack would also have happily blown the final whistle the second Wednesday took the lead. He constantly preached about keeping clean sheets and winning football matches 1-0. We even used to practice how to waste time in the closing minutes of a match by either hoofing or running the ball towards the corner flag. Entertainment was a dirty word.

It didn't take me long to realise just what I'd signed up for as we largely struggled through the final 15 league games. I signed on a Wednesday night in late March 1979, went back to Saints the following day to collect my stuff and say my goodbyes and had to be content with a place on the bench for my debut in a 1-0 defeat at Watford on the Saturday. My Hillsborough debut was a real culture shock. A few short weeks after playing against Forest at Wembley, I lined up against their Nottinghamshire neighbours Mansfield Town in front of half empty stands. There were only 11,065 watching us that day – a fairly typical Wednesday crowd that season – and to make it worse we got beaten 2-1. Without being disrespectful to my Wednesday team mates, it was never going to be easy to adjust to playing at a lower level or against clubs such as the Stags and Chester City, a team we scraped a 2-2 draw at a few weeks later in front of just 4,200 spectators. Boasting First Division facilities and potential also ensured Wednesday were an obvious target for smaller clubs who must have regarded coming to Hillsborough as a great day out and were always likely to raise their own game.

I did enjoy a happy Easter as Friday the 13th turned into a lucky day as I scored my first ever Wednesday goal in a 1-1 local derby draw against Hull City at Boothferry Park. Just 24 hours later we were back on home turf and Rodger Wylde helped himself to a couple of goals as we saw off Chesterfield 4-0. Those were rare highlights of a low key end to a mediocre season as Watford completed a quick-fire double with a 3-2 win at Hillsborough. Strangely, we finished the season with five successive home matches and, although we managed to put together three wins on the spin over Rotherham, Swindon and Blackpool, the final three attendances suggested

Wednesday fans couldn't wait for the season to end. All were under five figures with the lowest being the 7,310 who turned up to see us beat the Seasiders. We finished a disappointing 14th with just 45 points from our 46 matches – 15 points off the top three with Shrewsbury claiming the title and Watford and Swansea City also promoted. Best news on the blue horizon was that Sheffield United had been relegated from Division Two, so at least we were all set for two Steel City derbies in my first full season.

One worrying feature of my early time at Wednesday was a return of the pain below my knee. I'd forgotten about it after my first cortisone injection at Saints and didn't think there was much to worry about. The medics advised another injection – as they did in both of my next two seasons at Hillsborough. It was becoming obvious I had a problem and short term treatment was only masking the pain. But all I wanted to do was to get myself on the pitch and I didn't think at all about what affect it might have on me after my football days were finished.

I could hardly wait until August. The 1979-80 season was always going to be very special as here I was lining up for the club I idolised and with a mission to prove myself all over again. I'd lasted less than a couple of years combined at Derby and Southampton but was fired up to get Wednesday back on the right track after a few disappointing years. Each new season always begins with a lot of optimism – particularly if the club is as generally well supported as Wednesday – and we started well by defeating Hull City over two legs in the League Cup, with me scoring again in the away match.

We then kicked off our league campaign with a 3-0 win over Barnsley in front of more than 23,000 at Oakwell. There were a couple of contrasting players in the Tykes line up – Ronnie Glavin, the skilful Scottish midfielder and defender Mick McCarthy, later the Republic of Ireland, Sunderland and Wolves boss. As many of you will remember, Mick was a very hard tackling and uncompromising customer and I constantly wound him up by telling him he couldn't play. He wasn't very amused to say the least but I had the last laugh as I scored our first goal of the season. Barnsley was one of the away grounds – Luton and Millwall were two of the others – where I always got a lot of stick from the opposition fans. As my reputation as a club traveller spread, I'd be referred to as a 'gypo' – and, on occasions, a whole lot worse.

There's no denying being verbally abused for 90 minutes hurts and is quite difficult to deal with – after all, we're all flesh and blood and have feelings. On the other hand, as on that afternoon, it does wonders for your focus and determination to do well. I took being singled out for special attention as a compliment because they knew I was capable of doing damage to their team and just increased my efforts to make that happen. I knew I'd be in for plenty of verbals that campaign with a number of local sides including the Blades, Chesterfield, Rotherham United and Mansfield Town all in the Third Division.

Our weaknesses were fully exposed by a Blackburn Rovers side destined to be one of our main promotion rivals as they came to Hillsborough and won 3-0. They were handed a goal or two by Bob Bolder who had one of his off days. I remember the big man fumbling one effort onto the bar and then somehow failing to grab the rebound. Bolder enjoyed a good career, including a couple of seasons at Liverpool, but in my opinion was never particularly convincing at Wednesday. We came within eight minutes of a League Cup upset against Manchester City. We drew 1-1 at Hillsborough in the initial tie on a Tuesday night and were a goal up with time running out at Maine Road. Unfortunately City scored twice late on and we finished gallant losers. We then went on a local rollercoaster, getting a win at Millmoor over Emlyn Hughes' Rotherham United, drawing against Mansfield but losing 2-1 at a Chesterfield side well worth watching and allowing Barnsley to get revenge on us 2-0 at Hillsborough. My cheeky jibes at McCarthy came back to haunt me as the

Tykes battered us in the return and he wasn't slow to point out that I got what I deserved. As on many other occasions, I didn't do myself any favours by picking a needless argument with my direct opponent as it merely focused his attention on proving me wrong. I'd also like to admit this 34 years later: you really could play, Mick, I always recognised you were a good technical defender as well as a hard man.

It was high time for me to use my head as we looked for a much-needed victory against Grimsby Town on a Tuesday night at Hillsborough. My feet had been doing the business as I got myself onto the scoresheet quite regularly early in the season but Big Jack wasn't nearly so convinced how good I was in the air. As a striker, I used my head for talking; I was never very good at scoring goals with my bonce. Jack was so sure I couldn't nod one in he offered me £100 to prove him wrong – good bit of psychology that. Grimsby was the night when one of the lads managed to float one onto my head and I met it perfectly to send it soaring into the net. I've seen a photograph of the great event and I swear it was from just outside the penalty area! We won 2-0 and success rarely tasted so good. Big Jack's memory was never the best but I ensured he paid up – and confirmed the money was still up for grabs should I do it again. A few weeks later we were on the coast for the return game and getting beaten 3-1 with the fish and chips being scant consolation. It was that kind of up and down spell for us. We were doing no more than stay on the fringe of the promotion race come Christmas as a good 2-0 win victory at Reading took us back into sixth spot. To make things more urgent the Blades were top of the table.

Then came a very special occasion – the match for which I am best remembered – the Boxing Day clash with Sheffield United at Hillsborough. Sheffield is a very passionate football city and there are probably two measures of success as far as Wednesday fans are concerned: getting as high up the league as possible and beating the Blades. The build-up to the Steel City derby was something else. I was never bothered about all the pre-match hype or the kind to psyche myself up for kick off. The 90 minutes that followed was all the motivation I needed. But neither I nor any of the other lads could deny the Sheffield derby was special. There was nothing else on the radio, in the newspapers or being talked about down the pubs and clubs in the week leading up to it. Christmas Day 1979 was just the day before the really important event.

Losing the derby wasn't an option. There were several other true Wednesdayites in our squad, with Charlie Williamson and Mark Smith also in the starting line up on Boxing Day. After training each day, we piled into a nearby cafe to order a big fry-up and talk about what we were going to do to this or that United player. Kick off was brought forward to 11am on the advice of the City Council and there was no public transport that festive morning. But that didn't prevent the fans flocking to the ground in huge numbers. By 9.30am there were thousands outside Hillsborough, many of whom were never going to get in to watch the big game. Driving into the ground, I saw several thousands of fans milling around and more than 500 police trying their best to keep order. It was mayhem, to be honest.

In the dressing room an hour before the start, we were getting ourselves worked up. It all boiled down to one thing: we couldn't lose; we had to fight for every ball. Big Jack started his team talk: "Right, Mick Pickering; their lad up front, first chance you get, you rattle him. Then it's down to you, Mark Smith, you get in there and rattle him as well . . ." We set out to tempt players into retaliating and get sent off. Jack had no qualms about telling the lads to 'do' an opponent, then add: "Don't worry if you get booked or sent off: I'll have to say I'm fining you because the press will expect it, but I won't really. I'll make sure it's quashed."

By this time a huge crowd of 49,309 had packed into the ground creating an unbelievable atmosphere. It looked more like 60,000. In either case it was a record attendance for any Third Division match and remains so to this day. To give you another idea of just how special the Blades clash was we had just 11,530 and 13,287 fans for the home matches just before and after Boxing Day. The authorities did their best to ensure things didn't get out of hand. Someone came up with the idea the teams should walk out side by side before the game – something that only happened in the FA Cup final. Nice idea, but it nearly backfired as we lined up in the tunnel. John McPhail, one of the real Unitedites in their side, said he was going to break my leg; I just gave him a look before one of our players returned some verbals on my behalf. That led to all sorts of pushing and shoving with players from both sides squaring up and about to come to blows when the referee and linesmen stepped in and ordered us all onto the pitch. Tony Kenworthy also promised he would break my leg if I went anywhere near him and, like McPhail, looked as if he meant it!

The myth goes that I beat the Blades all on my own, which certainly wasn't the case. But it was one of my finest days. The game started relatively quietly before Ian Mellor sent a shockwave through both sets of passionate supporters with one of the best goals I've ever seen. He picked the ball up on the left side and sent a bullet-like shot beyond goalkeeper Derek Richardson from 25 yards. With both sides having chances, we were grateful to Bob Bolder for one great save and the woodwork for keeping us in front at half time.

Whatever Big Jack and United boss Harry Haslam said to the players, it was Wednesday who emerged from the traps the brighter for a dominant 45 minutes to elevate the match into local folklore. We'd already been denied a couple of times before a good run from McCulloch on the left side opened the way for my big moment after 63 minutes. I will always remember sending a flying header into the unguarded Blades net and setting off on my celebration. Sometimes you lose it completely and can hardly remember what you do afterwards. I sank to my knees in front of the Leppings Lane end in sheer ecstasy. I couldn't resist sliding towards the United fans –

not the most sensible thing to do but common sense goes out of the window. Some say scoring goals is better than sex – probably depends on who you've been out with.

I was pelted with hundreds of coins. I was on £300 a week and swear I'd have doubled that by picking them all up. To make the moment even more special that goal earned me another cool £100 off Big Jack. I could have had a second a couple of minutes later but instead rolled the ball across for Jeff King to tap in a simple third. By now we knew the game was ours and could almost relax and enjoy it. United were a beaten side well before the end and I also had a hand in the fourth goal as I went on a weaving run before being sent tumbling by Richardson in the Blades box for a clear penalty. The dependable Mark Smith duly beat Richardson from the spot – Sheffield Wednesday 4, Sheffield United 0, now that's Football Heaven! TC, the showman, came into play just before the end as I got the ball to take a corner at the Leppings Lane end and laid flat on my back, taking in a bit of unseasonal sun. The reaction of the Blades fans wasn't too friendly pelting more coins in my direction, but there was no danger of me getting into trouble with the boss. It doesn't matter what you do when you're 4-0 up, remember?

I was thrilled with the result and my performance. Leaving the pitch, I went up to McPhail and said: "I thought you were going to break my leg. You didn't even come close." Nothing could take the edge off the moment. There weren't showers in those days, just a big communal bath. We all sat there belting out the Boxing Day song that had been ringing around the ground minutes earlier – chorus after chorus of *Hark Now Hear the Wednesday Sing,* each louder than the last. Not a peep from the away dressing room. It was magical. Yet I hadn't a clue that more than 30 years later I'd still be remembered for that day. The game has reverberated through the ages and is still known as the Boxing Day massacre. Ask Wednesday fans their favourite derby memory and most will point to that festive feast rather than the 1993 FA Cup semi final when the Owls defeated the Blades 2-1 at Wembley. Even now I occasionally meet Wednesday fans who were there and relive the game. Memories are priceless and putting smiles on a lot of faces will always live with me. Writing this, I was once again swamped by newspaper journalists from the *Daily Mail*, the *Independent on Sunday* and *Yorkshire Post* getting me to re-tell my story as Wednesday prepared to go to Bramall Lane in 2011 for the first meeting between the two sides in the third flight since that famous season. It almost made me young again.

My actions were probably misunderstood by some Wednesday fans who thought I really hated the Blades. I'm not saying this to explain why I later joined United – that was a mistake I bitterly regret – but so you get a better idea what I'm about. I didn't show off because it was United we were playing; it could have happened anywhere, anytime. It was me being a showman, a big head in the best sense of the word. I enjoyed my football, including the odd chance to really entertain people and give them something to remember. I was extra hyped up because it was a big occasion and, with everything going my way, found an unusual way of celebrating and milking the moment. If I was disrespectful to the Blades, I apologise. Having said that, I probably paid for it a thousand times over when I played for United and their fans took it out on me. But, as far as the very real hatred that exists between Wednesday and United fans is concerned, I won't go there and never did. I'm no Mother Teresa but I just don't do hate; it's just not in my make-up. Of course, I was desperate to beat United that day and even listening on the radio to a Sheffield derby today, I'm desperate that Wednesday win as I want them to be successful and be the top team in the Steel City. But, derby days apart, I wish the Blades no harm.

For many fans, loving one club and hating another is part and parcel of the same thing. Having played for both Forest and Derby, been on the south coast where Saints and Pompey clash and on the edge of the Merseyside derby, I know where they are coming from. Providing dislike comes out in banter on radio phone-ins, in pubs or with mates that's brilliant. Football wouldn't be football without its rivalries, particularly in big cities such as Sheffield. But if it causes two people, who would get on fine if they met in an office or over a drink, to fight each other that's another thing altogether. I've never understood why people in big jobs turn into the most abusive yobs at a football match, yelling stuff you could never imagine coming out of educated mouths. Football violence has, thank goodness, become a lot rarer now than it was in the 1970s and 80s but, like racism, we shouldn't feel too comfortable until it is finished altogether.

Post Boxing Day I really pushed the boat out in style. It all started with getting an agent. There weren't too many around in the game but when a nice bloke called Gerry Webster from the insurance world approached me I could see it made sense. He promised to help me make more money and improve my career – sounded good to me. Little did he realise, though, that he'd be handling a 'pop star' as well!

It all started when I was approached by Alan Wood, from Jimmy James and the Vagabonds – the group that brought us *Now Is the Time* and *Red Red Wine* to name just two of their hits. Alan asked if I'd like to record a special version of *Singing the Blues*, another classic that has been recorded by some very big names after first being released in 1956. Suddenly I'd have something in common with Guy Mitchell and Tommy Steele. I did point out one small issue to Alan: I can't sing! "Don't worry," he replied. "We can do virtually anything in the recording studio, so we can make you sound good!"

I was warming to the idea but there were a couple of things I wasn't keen on. Alan's a big Wednesday fan and wanted me to sing a chorus of 'when Wednesday win and United lose . . .' But, because of the hooligan problem in football and the bitter rivalry between the two Sheffield clubs, I didn't want to be accused of making the situation even worse. Alan also told me there was a good way of ensuring my record got high in the charts and could even appear on *Top of the Pops*. The weekly chart was decided by sales of records from a select number of shops and Alan said they could bus people into Leicester, London, Manchester and Newcastle to buy my record. But again I didn't think that was on.

I really enjoyed the recording though. Alan got the Chuck Fowler Band to accompany me and we had a great day at a recording studio in Hull. We set out at 9am and came back home at 2am after a full day's work and plenty of fun. Soon afterwards *Singing the Blues* was played for the first time at Hillsborough before kick off, beginning a tradition that has continued to this day. Big Jack thought it was a good laugh but, as you can imagine, the lads weren't slow to take the mickey out of me. It sold around 3,500 copies, despite me not choosing to flood the chart shops, and was popular on one side of Sheffield at least. United fans weren't quite as keen with one Blades fan bidding £1,700 on a radio station just to blow it up!

I'm so pleased I recorded that song because, as with the Boxing Day massacre, it has always lived with me. Early in 2010 memories were brought back to life when I attended a concert by Paul Carrick, the Sheffield-based singer of Mike and the Mechanics fame. He invited me onto the stage at Brighouse to sing the song all over again. I really enjoyed myself and was pleased to find out my voice is still in a lot better shape than my knackered knees. There was even talk about re-recording it.

If singing wasn't enough, I then got myself a fan club. Gerry and I talked about the fact I was getting quite a lot of mail, including plenty from admiring females. So we decided to give the staff at Hillsborough a break and open an official Terry Curran fan club to deal with it all properly. In truth I didn't have a great deal to do with it. Gerry answered all the letters and I let him get on with it. I didn't even use it as a way of meeting more women because there was no point. Each time I'd emerge from the players' entrance at Hillsborough there'd be women calling out, telling me what they'd like to do. So I had no problem meeting Wednesday fans if I wanted to. The fan club ran until I left Hillsborough a couple of seasons later.

The most significant thing about the Boxing Day massacre was the amazing affect one result seemed to have on the two clubs. We went from strength to strength despite losing our next Hillsborough match against Plymouth Argyle whilst the Blades simply slumped. Starting with a 2-2 draw at Brentford, we went on a dazzling 16-match unbeaten run to put us well on course for promotion. Bury and Rotherham were both hit for five during an eight-game spell in which we defied Jack's orders and couldn't stop scoring goals – 25 in all. This golden period co-incided with Jack pushing me up front alongside Andy McCulloch, a partnership I always thought would work well. Good mates off the pitch, we worked well together on it as Andy was big and strong and put in a lot of hard work and I had the pace and trickery to take full advantage. I helped myself to nine goals in 12 matches – probably the most productive spell of my professional career – with Andy not far behind.

Successive derbies with Chesterfield and Rotherham United were memorable for several reasons. The Spireites were having a very good run of their own and came to Hillsborough still very much in the hunt for promotion. With the match going deeper and deeper into injury time, it looked as if we were going to claim a vital two points as we led 3-2 despite their goalkeeper Mark Kendall making a penalty save from the normally reliable Mark Smith. Chesterfield folklore suggests it was about six o'clock when Geoff Salmons, the former Blades player, popped up with a last gasp equaliser that could so easily have been critical come the end of the season. I ended that long afternoon by having a slight argument in the tunnel with Bill Green, the rugged Spireites centre half I'd first started warring with at Forest when he was a Carlisle man. Worse was to follow in the dressing room as an angry

Big Jack laid into me for not following his instructions and running the ball into the corner as the game went into injury time.

I got my revenge in an usual manner when Rotherham United were thrashed 5-0 at Hillsborough seven days later. Just before the interval with us already well in command, I picked up the ball on the edge of the Millers' penalty area, turned back and ran all the way to our own corner flag to howls of derision from Owls fans. Jack was totally bemused at half time and asked what the hell I was doing. "That was for you, Jack," I replied cheekily. "You love defensive football!" You ought to have seen the look on his face, particularly as several of the other Wednesday lads saw the funny side. More seriously, that was a great afternoon for the emerging McCulloch-Curran partnership as Andy helped himself to a hat trick and I scored as well. Our convincing success also took us into the top three – and therefore the promotion places – for the first time since the opening couple of games. With more than 20,000 flocking into Hillsborough for both derbies, life couldn't get much better – yet it did!

Successive 2-0 away victories over Carlisle United and Oxford United took us to within sniffing distance of top spot and set me up for the next fixture at Hillsborough against struggling Wimbledon and a weekend I will never forget – although not all for footballing reasons. To make sense of this story, allow me to go back to October and the first clash between the two sides at 'glamorous' Plough Lane. Quite an afternoon it was, too, with two leaky defences allowing seven goals – Wednesday won 4-3 and I got two of them. But the real fun started in the bar afterwards. I was enjoying a quiet drink with the lads when this gorgeous blonde, who turned out to be the girlfriend of one of the Wimbledon lads, made a decidedly 'sexist' remark in my direction. At first, I allowed it to go over my head but the young woman made it quite clear she would love to see me when the two teams played again – no doubt to compare a few tactical formations between the sheets. Then, to make sure I got the message, she slipped her phone number into my pocket.

I've been known to lose and forget a few things – especially in later life – but never a woman's telephone number! I kept it safe and gave her a buzz a few days before Wimbledon were due to come up to Sheffield in early March to see if she was going to keep her sexy promise. "Yes, of course," she said, telling me to meet her off the train on the Friday afternoon. I needed a long and credible pass out to satisfy my wife and told her that Jack had ordered the whole team to stay together in a hotel that evening in preparation for the game. This was something the First Division clubs I played for sometimes did although, in truth, Wednesday only stayed overnight for away games and used the Rutland Hotel for pre-match meals when we were at Hillsborough. I booked a room at the Rutland with my mind on anything but the football.

I turned up at Sheffield railway station at about 3pm still not knowing quite what to expect. Imagine my thoughts when I saw her running towards me in her delicious fur coat, made even more special with just sexy white suspenders beneath. Wow, Terry, you're onto a winner here, I thought to myself (or something like that!). Obviously I'm not going to go into all the ups and downs but, let's say, this match certainly lived up to expectations. All those kicks and bruises you get from being a footballer are well worthwhile when it helps pull a bird like her! Not exactly textbook preparation for Saturday's match, but who was complaining? Uncovering the sexy secrets beneath that fur coat was worth any flak that could have come my way.

Without writing a porno, we made love throughout the rest of the afternoon and long into the evening. The hours flashed by without us really noticing. We were then celebrating with a bath when the evening took an unexpected twist. It was well after midnight when we heard a firm knock on our hotel room door that simply wouldn't go away. Eventually, I did the gentlemanly thing by wrapping a towel around me and answering it. "Sorry, sir, we would advise you to get dressed and meet down in reception," said the hotel porter. "What's the matter?" I asked, a little baffled. "There's been an incident nearby and we need everyone out of their rooms and into the car park," he added. There we were standing alongside the other guests wondering what on earth was happening when I spotted two policemen I knew from match days at Hillsborough. One gave me the shock news that the Yorkshire Ripper, of all people, had been arrested a few hundred yards away! Of course, it turned out to be really good news as that evil monster Peter Sutcliffe had haunted South Yorkshire women for a couple of years with fear spreading throughout the area that a serial killer was on the loose. But I had more mundane things on my mind. I knew I shouldn't have been there and was desperate the policemen didn't tip off Big Jack about my pre-match frolics. They assured me they wouldn't say a word and I heard no more about it.

Jack caught me out with women a couple of times, including when he and his wife Pat came across me and a young lady they knew wasn't my wife in a Sheffield shopping centre, so I was just grateful to get away scot free. The Wimbledon woman and I said our goodbyes with me promising her an appropriate on-field performance.

It's not easy to follow sex with a bombshell, but a hat trick would have been nice. I never tried harder in my life to get one – anything to put on a good show for my secret blonde! I got my first goal just before half time after fastening onto a miscued clearance and, when I outran a defender to score again midway through the second half, time was on my side. I looked at the Hillsborough clock showing ten minutes past four and was convinced I could get another one at least. I chased everything in a bid to score my first professional treble – at one point I got tripped and, instead of doing the professional thing and staying down for a free kick, I went after the ball on my knees. I had to admit defeat in my one-man mission as we couldn't add to our 3-1 lead but victory took one of my teams to the top of the league for the first time in my career – and the second time I'd been 'on top' inside 24 hours! I never did score a professional hat trick and Big Jack never found out what really motivated his striker to perform out of his skin. Until now. Pity she couldn't have come to Hillsborough every week!

Successive 1-1 draws at Mansfield Town's Field Mill, which was packed to the rafters, and Gillingham, kept the pot boiling nicely before Blackpool rolled into town for the next Hillsborough fixture. This was another great afternoon for me as I banged in another couple of goals – one from the edge of the penalty area, the other after cutting in from the left flank – as we roared to a 4-1 victory to take us back to top place. Amazingly that made it 20 goals in just five Hillsborough matches and we were beginning to think we were invincible.

There was still reason for Big Jack to be cautious, however, when we followed up a 1-1 draw at Southend United by being held at home by the same scoreline by Reading despite my goal. Four draws in five put more pressure on the return Sheffield derby at Bramall Lane. The build up was almost equally as intense as Boxing Day with roles having now been largely reversed. We were the team sitting in the top three on the back of a long unbeaten run with the Blades almost in the last chance saloon. Victory over their great rivals would keep them in with half a shout of promotion as well as gain some consolation for the Boxing Day massacre.

Once again the match drew a very large crowd and was one of the very few Third Division games featured on *Match of the Day*. The early stages didn't go to our script as United drew first blood and their goalkeeper Terry Poole kept us at bay with some good saves. Meanwhile I ensured the TV men had plenty to get their teeth stuck into afterwards by having a running battle with United's Tony Kenworthy. Blades boss Harry Haslam clearly decided I wasn't going to get the freedom of Bramall Lane after my success on Boxing Day and got his best defender to mark me. That meant following me everywhere on the pitch, kicking me as far in the air as possible and generally ensuring I was too knackered to cause any damage. I respected Tony as a very good player and he quickly let me know he was there by getting in a couple of crunching tackles. Welcome to Bramall Lane, TC! Later in the first half I got my revenge with a 'mistimed' challenge on Kenworthy before mockingly slapping him around the chops, saying: "See how you like it, mate, not nice being kicked is it?" He responded angrily and a few moments later the United defender was spread-eagled on the deck with the finger of suspicion being pointed at Blades' public enemy number one. Luckily, the referee didn't see too much in the incident and I stayed on the pitch. It was so obvious how closely Kenworthy was watching me that when I went to the toilet at half time one of the Wednesday lads shouted: "Where's your marker, TC?"

Into the second half and United were still leading 1-0 with time beginning to run out. It was going to need some magic to prevent the home side from getting back some of the local bragging rights and it was me who came up with it. When I received the ball near the left corner flag, I had more than Kenworthy for company as I was surrounded by red and white stripes and had no idea what I was going to do. I set off back towards the edge of the area leaving three defenders in my wake, got the ball onto my right foot and let rip – a dream 20-yard angled shot that soared high past Terry Poole and into the back of the United net. I still insist my goal for Forest against Fulham was better, but many Wednesday fans will disagree. Legendary BBC commentator Barry Davies came out with the words: "Whatever you think about Terry Curran, when he puts his mind to it this boy can play!" Thanks Barry for the compliment but I was never like that. Perhaps because I was always attempting the spectacular and attracted tight markers, I had more than my fair share of quieter games – but it was never for the want of trying.

The game finished 1-1 which suited us more than them and

so to the post-match inquest, led naturally by Jimmy Hill. Both Tony and I were interviewed by Barry and played down the incident that was in any case largely handbags at dawn. Yes, I did tap Tony by the ankles but I certainly didn't stamp on him – nor would I ever have done. It was good to hear Tony say he respected me, too, as a player and we would enjoy a drink and a laugh about the incident in the bar afterwards. That took the wind out of Jimmy Hill's sails who concluded it was good to hear two professionals speak like that.

Performing in a huge match in front of the TV cameras was great but Jack knew the bread and butter games were going to be just as important if we were to get promotion. Just two nights after Bramall Lane we struggled on our own patch against plucky Gillingham – but again just one moment of personal inspiration got us out of jail. I picked the ball up in midfield and ran at the Gills, getting past three defenders before I was sent crashing. Mark Smith strode up to win the match for us with the only goal from the penalty spot. It's difficult to describe what it feels like when you are on such a long unbeaten run. It doesn't matter which division you are in, being successful breeds confidence and you just can't wait for Saturday to come. When you run out onto the pitch, you're not worried about your opponents, you just know you are going to do well. That was what it was like with Wednesday. We honestly thought our momentum would take us to the end of the season and get us over the finishing line with something to spare, yet we were in for a rude shock. A single goal defeat at Bury in our 42nd league game ensured a top three finish was by no means certain.

We responded well by beating Chester at Hillsborough 3-0. The visitors included a couple of very interesting names with a young Ian Rush playing up front just before moving to Liverpool for £300,000 and becoming a goalscoring legend. On the right wing was a poor bloke by the name of Peter Sutcliffe, who probably got enough of a ribbing from fans for being a namesake of the infamous serial killer – so I'll leave him alone.

Next came a crucial Tuesday night at Ewood Park. Blackburn were almost promoted whilst we couldn't afford to allow them to repeat their triumph in Sheffield. It was a tense, exciting evening that ended perfectly with me getting on the scoresheet and Wednesday winning 2-1. I ran up the railings behind the goal in sheer joy – I swear I almost hung myself!

The script was set fair for us to go to Exeter City on the Saturday, take the two points and celebrate promotion. Another sizeable Owls following, outnumbering home fans in a crowd of just over 10,000, clearly thought the same way. But City were in the top eight and certainly no pushovers and, with Smudger missing from the spot, we went down by a single goal. Yet the day still ended in glory as news came through that our nearest challengers Chesterfield had also failed to win and we were all but mathematically in the Second Division with just the visit of Carlisle United to come. We were two points clear and had a superior goal difference of 12 so there was no way anyone could wreck our promotion party. Directors brought champagne into the dressing room and the celebration was long and special. Usually, a journey home after losing at Exeter would be one of the most boring and depressing in football, but I swear we didn't care a jot.

I'd played at Wembley and was later part of an Everton team that won the First Division title, but this was undoubtedly one of the best moments of my football life. It may have only been the Third Division in other people's eyes but, as a player and a fan, this meant everything. After so many years in the wilderness, Wednesday weren't so much back where we belonged – I will always maintain that is the top flight – but on the right track. Despite being a big club, we didn't have any divine right to get promoted and it had taken five long seasons and much heartache before we gave our loyal supporters a hint of success. So why not enjoy it?

That fantastic feeling lasted way beyond the following

Saturday when more than 32,000 came to Hillsborough for the last match of the season against Carlisle United – an afternoon all about the occasion rather than the actual performance. Just as well as an uneventful 90 minutes ended without a goal. The final table showed just how close the promotion race had been. We finished in the third and final promotion slot with 58 points, just one ahead of Chesterfield, with Blackburn and champions Grimsby joining us in the higher flight. Amazingly, the Blades only took 16 points after Christmas to finish in mid-table with 46 points from 46 games – and 12 months later were staring Fourth Division football in the face. It's unbelievable how quickly fortunes can change in this game.

Clinching promotion in my first full season with Wednesday was also one in the eye for the critics who lambasted me for dropping down two leagues. I was also delighted to become the Third Division's Golden Boot as I finished top scorer with 22 goals from 41 starts. Add in my two League Cup goals against Hull City and 24 was by far the best season of my career and justified my belief that being an out and out striker was my best position. Considering Mark Smith took all the penalties that term, I could easily have topped 30.

6

Rollercoaster with Big Jack and my Biggest Regret

LIFE for me in Sheffield couldn't have been much better with promotion on the field and a fantastic social life off it. I was still married to Kim but never let that cramp my style. I don't want to be disrespectful to her here but, as I've already said, I just wasn't good husband material. I enjoyed going out on the town with the Wednesday lads but, as on the field, used different tactics to most of my mates. They got themselves blind drunk, then tried to find themselves a young lady; I concentrated on the main job in hand of finding a bird. Better to wake up with a girl on your arm than a hangover in your head, I thought.

On the pitch I wanted to score goals, off it my 'goal' was getting myself a shag. Well, at least I'm honest enough to admit it. Whether out on my own or with the lads, I scoured the room for a decent looking young woman who seemed to be on her own. Blonde, brunette, tall, small, it didn't really matter. As long as they looked nice and wanted some fun that was fine by me. It helps when you aren't worried about being rejected. Some of the lads, even though well known and liked in the city, were too shy to talk to a woman in case she wasn't interested. Not TC. To me, it was similar to being in the first team. If a woman didn't want me I'd move on to someone who did, like I moved clubs. Sounds a bit harsh but there's always more fish in the sea, as they say. I didn't need alcohol to give me Dutch courage. I sipped my coke – sometimes between 25 and 35 bottles on a particularly long night – and chatted.

Being free from drink meant I concentrated on the woman I was talking to. I was good looking, in my prime and loved the company of young women. How many men wouldn't do exactly the same if they had the chance? My favourite pulling haunt in Sheffield was a night club called Josephine's. It's no longer around these days but, back then, it was arguably the city's top night spot – big, brash, playing the latest chart music and, most importantly, packed with lovely looking women. Being a footballer and easily recognisable was a great icebreaker, particularly if the young woman came from the right side of Sheffield. It didn't bother me, however, if she couldn't tell me from Adam. That way she wouldn't be aware of my reputation as a football-playing womaniser!

Some went to bed with me the first night we met; others took two or three weeks. I considered it time well spent if I got there in the end. Everything was about the chase; the excitement of the unknown. My marriage was a sham, but I wasn't in the market for a long term relationship and made that very clear. I wanted sexual adventure and that was it. Do I live that way now? No, I don't. Do I regret the way I lived then? I enjoyed it but I'm certainly not proud of the way I treated Kim. There were girls I kept my distance from as they could have got too attached. I was lucky or hard enough to enjoy the moment without falling for any of them. Being married actually helped in a strange way. It meant either going to her place or booking a hotel room, adding to the sexual excitement and anticipation.

Sometimes we weren't the only guests having fun. There were nights resembling the so-called 'roasting' sessions for which footballers have made headlines in recent years. This is when one woman has sex with a group of men. We never went out intending that to happen. But sometimes we'd only pull one woman between us. If we were all booked into the same hotel – as during an away trip for example – sometimes we'd ask whether the woman minded the other boys watching while she had sex. Providing she was up for that, next step was to ask her if she'd like to have sex with one or more of the others.

Don't get me wrong, I realise how easily this can become abusive. But I was never part of anything like that. The women we met were as happy to take part as we were. Some just love the thrill of sex with more than one person. What happened was all good mutual fun. Nobody got hurt or, if they did, they were very good actresses. I can't speak for the women involved in the events that have hit the newspapers – but rape and sexual abuse is terrible and when that's the case the footballers deserve all they get. But it is too easy for girls, with unreturned feelings or guilty about what has gone on, to cash in by selling a story to the highest bidder. Today's top footballers are a much easier and more obvious target as they live such a glamorous lifestyle.

My typical night out after a Saturday home match ended about 6am with me crawling back home to Kim. The fact she put up with it – or turned a blind eye – for so long shows what an unequal relationship we had. Kim tried everything she could to keep our marriage on track and I carried on creating more and more problems. I'm not proud of that but I was just being me – a young man living in my own sexual candy shop. If I could turn the clock back, I wouldn't have got married and hurt a woman who deserved so much better.

As you may have guessed, I wasn't too keen on the 'no sex' rule the night before a match that managers usually imposed. I didn't argue with it because too much athletic activity isn't going to help you much the following afternoon and you don't want players out on the town with women on a Friday night. But when you're safely tucked up at home with the missus, as on most Friday nights during my career, the temptation was often too much. I'd reserve my clubbing for after a game when I was still high on excitement and didn't think it was going to do any harm either to myself or the team.

Our elation at getting promotion lasted all the way to the kick off of the 1980-81 season – but it was becoming obvious

Big Jack and I weren't quite singing from the same hymn sheet. He made it clear he was going to give the same squad the chance to prove themselves in the Second Division and was looking for us to consolidate at the higher level. I considered the job at Wednesday only half done and wanted to see Big Jack bring in new faces to boost our chances of making another promotion challenge. We may have been meeting up again with famous clubs such as Newcastle United, Chelsea and West Ham United but surely we wanted to get into the First Division as quickly as possible?

We enjoyed a nice bonus before kicking a ball in the league when we again disposed of the Blades, this time in the first round of the League Cup. The tie was played over two legs and I had two more good games to make myself even more unpopular with Blades fans. I set up first half goals for Kevin Taylor and Jeff Johnson as we began with all guns blazing at Hillsborough before the Blades gave us a much tougher second half without being able to get a goal. They did, however, reduce the deficit by scoring first at Bramall Lane before I burst forward to net a second half equaliser to ensure there was no way back. It finished 1-1 with the Owls winning 3-1 on aggregate.

We opened the league season in fine style with a 2-0 home win over Newcastle and I had the perfect draw in the second round of the League Cup – Wimbledon! We lost 2-1 at Plough Lane and I managed to set eyes on my secret blonde. We exchanged knowing smiles recalling the great time we had shared, but there was never going to be a chance of a replay. We triumphed 3-1 in the return to book our place in round three 4-3 on aggregate.

Wednesday were still riding the promotion wave in early September when an afternoon at Oldham's Boundary Park brought Terry Curran and the club to national attention for all the wrong reasons. There was a typically large and vocal following from Wednesday on a red hot day and the incident everyone was talking about afterwards unfortunately happened right in front of them. It didn't help that the referee was George Courtney, an official who seemed to have my number. I was sent off five or six times in my professional career and it was almost always Courtney in the middle. He obviously got it into his head I was a bad egg – and I can't blame him for that – but this time he got the big decision totally wrong. We were attacking the Oldham goal and their striker Simon Stainrod chased back to kick the ball out for a throw. I wanted to take it quickly but was stopped from doing so as he pushed me in the chest. I then brought my knee up with the idea of getting him where it really hurts. We were close together but I had time to stop and avoid making contact with him. Next moment Stainrod was rolling around on the ground as if I had caught him. I don't know where the linesman was but Courtney walked towards me and brought out a card from his pocket. When we both saw it was red, Stainrod jumped to his feet and started laughing. The fans went ballistic. I shouted at Stainrod that he was a 'fucking cheat' but it wasn't going to make any difference. I had to go.

Stainrod was a guy who, like me, played his football with a fairly short fuse; a Sheffield lad turned down as a youngster by his boyhood club Wednesday, he played for the Blades before going to Oldham. He wasn't popular with Owls fans and that was magnified a thousand times that sad day.

I didn't see what happened next because I was on my way back to the dressing room. The first time I saw fans coming onto the pitch and hurling objects was on the TV news that night. There was a lot of rubble on the terraces in the stand hosting the Owls fans who picked up concrete and stones and hurled debris onto the pitch making a bad incident a whole lot worse. Big Jack came out onto the pitch to try to restore order and nearly copped it himself. I remember seeing him crying in the dressing room because he was so ashamed of what happened. It was the first time I'd ever seen a grown man reduced to tears and upset me even more. The game was held up for about half-an-hour before Oldham completed a

2-0 victory.

My punishment was to be hauled up in front of a specially convened FA tribunal with a nervous Jack Charlton by my side. Chairman of the panel was Bert Millichip who looked like a typical headteacher ready to give me the cane. I was eager to lace into him and tell him my case but Big Jack tapped my ankles under the table to tell me to keep quiet. The verdict was a month's suspension for me – one match for the sending off and three for going over the points limit. Wednesday had to play our next few games at Hillsborough with the terraces closed. Chairman Bert McGhee pulled me in to give me a further rollicking but I stopped him in his tracks. "I didn't do anything wrong and the club's takings are going to increase over the next four games because fans who usually stand will have seats instead," I argued. Hearing that, he stopped the rollicking and seemed quite satisfied. His smile widened still further as the empty terraces failed to halt our good early form.

Stressful times such as that show you who your friends are. Although I'd done nothing to provoke the riot, my reputation as a hot-heated, unpredictable so-and-so meant plenty of people were pleased to see me in trouble. Yet Bally took the time and effort to stand up for me, writing in the papers that, although excitable, I was an honest lad who would have been horrified by what happened. He added that Saints had made a big mistake by allowing me to go to Wednesday and he'd have me in his Blackpool team tomorrow. That gave me a real boost when I needed it most. In another good piece of timing, I received my award for being the leading goalscorer in Division Three a few days later from Jimmy Hill. Standing alongside Phil Boyer, my former Saints colleague, who took the First Division prize, and Clive Allen, Division Two top scorer with QPR, helped take my mind off the Oldham incident and reminded me I was a good footballer.

I sat out my four games and couldn't wait to get back into action again in the night match against Blackburn Rovers when the terraces ban was still in force. Sometimes you have a funny feeling you're going to score and I certainly did that night. I hadn't got off the mark that season and was more than ready to put that right: cue a very special TC goal celebration! McCulloch flicked on a long clearance just before half time and I turned past my marker before lobbing the ball over goalkeeper John Butcher for the winner. Instinctively, I kept running and sank to my knees to celebrate in front of a totally empty Kop end! Wednesday photographer Steve Ellis took a great snap and it still makes me laugh when I think about it. Nobody could accuse me of inciting the fans.

Next fireworks came from Big Jack just after Bonfire Night and was one of the first signs of what was set to become an on and off running battle with the boss. I scored both goals, including a penalty and a late winner, to see off Wrexham 2-1 at Hillsborough. But Jack had a real go in the press, claiming he'd had to gee me up at half time because I'd been sulking. He didn't want to play me in my preferred position alongside Andy McCulloch because I couldn't play with my back to goal. I said I'd be off if he continued to play me in a nowhere position. I meant it, too, but things settled down again. There would be many twists and turns before our relationship finally broke down.

I enjoyed another distraction from the football by getting myself a greyhound. I'd always been interested in the dogs since my Kinsley days and, being at Wednesday and near a track at Owlerton, provided me with the perfect chance to get back into it. Andy McCulloch and I heard about a dog called Spiral Please and decided to take the plunge. Big Jack wanted a piece of it as well, so we all chipped in £600 to buy the beast for £1,800. It was trained by Harry Crapper at Owlerton. All was looking good as Spiral Please won his first race. Our dog was then ready to race on the Saturday when I got a call to tell me he had picked up an injury. I told Harry I'd pick it up and take it to Hillsborough for infra red treatment. He didn't believe me at first, but went along with it. The funny thing was that Mel Sterland, one of the younger lads in the Wednesday side, was on the treatment table when I got Spiral Please to Hillsborough. He was trying to get himself fit to play in an important match on the same day as the big race. You ought to have seen the look of disbelief on Mel's face when I burst in with the dog and told him to get off the table. "This is far more important," I told him. "We need the dog for Saturday!" To his credit, Mel took it in great heart. He liked a flutter himself, saw the comical side and probably realised that, as Big Jack was a co-owner, it was difficult to argue. It proved a mixed weekend: the dog was passed fit and lost; Mel somehow made the weekend game and we won! That was the beginning of the end for poor Spiral Please – the dog never quite recaptured that first race form and we eventually lost faith in what the trainers were telling us and decided to call it a day. It was fun while it lasted and worthwhile just for that one incident with Mel!

That wasn't the end for me with greyhounds as I also owned my own while at Wednesday. I bought one particularly distinctive dog called Darkie for £500 to race on the flapping tracks. Darkie came up trumps in his first race at Kinsley but I was wary that, if my dog became too well recognised, I wouldn't get very good odds for his next race at Whitwood. Bookmakers looked out for owners who were quite well known and would presume it was an expensive dog with a good chance of winning. So I asked Steve Ellis whether he could look after it for me. Steve knew nothing about greyhounds but being a great guy was happy to help me out. You ought to have seen the look on his face when he came to my house in Cudworth to pick up Darkie and saw me dying the beast's feet black with hair dye. He asked what on earth I was doing and I explained I didn't want the bookies to know this was my dog.

I kept out of the way in my van on race day leaving Steve to prepare Darkie for the race. The dog was temperamental, being a puller when out walking, and a sprinter who might struggle to last the distance. Problem was that unknown to me Darkie, who was in race three, went ballistic in Steve's van hearing the bell for the first two and virtually ran two races before getting to the starting line! Steve, bless him, took Darkie into the parade ring, struggling to get his muzzle on and putting on his coat back to front whilst I was studying the odds. We opened at 7-4 and I handed over £1,000 to a couple of mates to back Darkie although the bookies only accepted £500. Darkie was evens when the race started and was never in contention after a bad collision at the first bend. All that wasted energy hadn't helped. It didn't put me off though and I continued to be attracted by the gambling side of greyhound racing until my move to Sheffield United. I still have an interest now as my brother John owns the Kinsley track.

Big Jack surprised me when he pulled me aside and asked a strange question apparently out of the blue: "Have you ever thought about playing for Scotland?" Well, my Dad and grandfather were both Scottish so, yes, I could have represented the Tartan Army but I was 100 per cent English and playing for my country was one of my main ambitions. Scotland, the only home nation who'd definitely qualified for the 1982 World Cup in Spain, had been in touch with Big Jack to check on my availability.

Later when Big Jack became the most popular of adopted Irishmen he got quite a reputation for thinking outside of the Republic and persuading folk like Ray Houghton, Jason McAteer and Tony Cascarino to name just three that they should play for the country. Rumour had it he even tried to persuade Stan Collymore he was Irish. Perhaps it was Scotland's enquiry about me that set him on this course? I've no regrets about saying no, even though I never got a sniff with England despite Big Jack, ironically, doing his best to recommend me. Although I loved my Dad and it would have made him very proud, my heart was with England. Simple as that really. I don't have any particular argument with players who take the opposite view and cash in on their parentage to represent other countries. You should always try to play at the highest level if, at all possible, so if lads feel they won't get an England call and choose to represent Wales, Scotland or one of the Irish teams, good luck to them. It just wasn't right for me.

Another interesting feature that season was that our record signing, Ante Mirocevic, also became Wednesday's first ever overseas player. The midfielder had already created history by becoming the first player from Montenegro to represent Yugoslavia and came to Hillsborough with a big reputation. It wasn't entirely new ground for me as I'd played with another Yugoslavian international, Ivan Golac, at Saints and was a subject I'd written about in my column in the Sheffield Star. When I forecast more foreign players and even managers would come into English football some people probably thought I'd be expecting Martians to land next, but this was the start of a trend that has added greatly to our football. Ante got mixed press during his spell at Wednesday and the communication gap – he didn't speak good English – certainly didn't help. But I learned a lot from playing with someone who had so much technical skill and was, if anything, too good for Wednesday rather than the other way round.

Five wins out of six took us to within a couple of points of early leaders West Ham in October and our Hillsborough form – with or without the terraces – was so good it wasn't until Orient became our seventh visitors that we surrendered any home points from a 2-2 draw. Everything was looking good yet the FA were getting their knickers in a twist about another huge issue – goal celebrations! There was too much kissing and hugging, they said, not like the 'good old days' when proper men exchanged a formal handshake after scoring. Goodness knows what damage they thought it was causing society. It was a talking point in our dressing room before the home game against Bristol Rovers just before Christmas. I made Ian Mellor laugh by saying if I scored I'd run back to the centre circle and take a gentle bow to all four stands. He knew I was the one person in the team who would actually do it. Andy McCulloch helped himself to a couple of goals and Mark Smith was on target, too, but it was my goal the fans probably remember as I ignored the lads rushing to congratulate me and did the gentlemanly thing to all sides of Hillsborough.

That was my way of making a point in an entertaining way but, in truth, the whole thing showed how out-of-touch these guys were. There's no feeling in the world like scoring a goal, whether playing in front of a couple of hundred or 100,000 fans. Your head explodes with excitement and you go into a different world. The fans are excited and want to celebrate with you – and you want to celebrate with them. Goals are what football is all about and, if you can't get excited when you score, you might as well spend Saturday afternoons shopping. I may have occasionally celebrated in front of the opposition supporters but meant no harm. I was so swept away by the moment I didn't know or care where I was, let alone what I was doing. Today hugging and kissing is back and goal celebrations are many and varied. Yet officials still try their best to take the fun out of them by issuing pointless bookings when goalscorers take their shirts off – although I'm still not sure why players insist on doing so. We should encourage every ounce of excitement and celebration we can in this game of ours.

The Rovers victory meant we went into Christmas in a more than handy fifth spot that could have been even better had we not been held to a 1-1 Boxing Day draw by Shrewsbury Town. For much of the rest of that 1980-81 season a second successive promotion was still very much on the cards despite the fact the Hammers were now pulling away at the top and Notts County, who inflicted a rare 2-1 Hillsborough defeat on us, were always favourites to join them.

Big Jack's disciplinary procedures also got increasingly strange as the cracks started to widen between us. He hauled me into his office to fine me £100 for getting booked for dissent against Bristol City. I told him there was no way I was going to pay it as I disputed the caution in the first place. So Jack came up with a comical compromise so he could tell the press he had dealt with me. He asked his assistant John Harris to go into the safe and fish out £100 for me. Then Big Jack asked me to give it him back. Honestly, that's exactly what happened!

Successive victories over Oldham Athletic – a game in which I exacted revenge by helping myself to a couple of goals – Swansea City and Queen's Park Rangers lifted us into the third promotion spot with just 12 matches to play. We remained there even though draws against Cardiff City and Derby County slightly halted our momentum. The Derby game, played in front of more than 28,000 fans at Hillsborough, was better remembered for another example of my showmanship that seriously wound up Big Jack. I dribbled around the goalkeeper and, instead of simply passing the ball into the net, sank down on my knees and headed it in. The manager went ballistic, ranting and raving on the touchline and giving me a really hard time when I got back into the dressing room. The irony was the 'goal' was chalked off for offside! It wasn't my day as I also missed a spot kick as try as we might we couldn't break the deadlock.

During the following week, we had an interesting visitor – Sheffield-born entertainer Michael Palin, a big Wednesday fan. He was very popular as part of *Monty Python's Flying Circus*, a very original comedy programme that really made me laugh. We sat together in the Hillsborough dressing room to have a chat and have our photo taken. He did his best to keep my spirits up after Derby by pointing out he had plenty of days at the 'office' when things didn't exactly go to plan. I thought it strange why such a well-known person wanted to meet a bunch of footballers. How things have changed as nowadays footballers are the celebrities and other famous people flock around them. I enjoyed meeting Michael as I did other VIP Wednesday fans such as Labour MPs Roy Hattersley, a regular at Hillsborough for many years, and

David Blunkett as well as singer Paul Carrick.

Palin's psychology didn't quite do the trick as we then went to Blackburn Rovers and failed to repeat our heroics of a few months before. That 3-1 defeat, plus another loss against Orient, made it all the more important we disposed of David Pleat's talented Luton Town side when the *Match of the Day* cameras came to Hillsborough on April 4. Mirocevic gave us a first half lead before I tucked away two chances in rapid succession after the break to virtually wrap up the points. The 3-1 victory left us just one point outside of the promotion frame with a game in hand on third placed Swansea City.

The shit really hit the fan seven days later when we travelled to Wales with every confidence we could get another victory at Wrexham and really step up our challenge. We were never at the races at the Racecourse Ground and got well and truly turned over 4-0. Big Jack was becoming known for his post match inquests and really laid into us that afternoon. Flying tea cups, often with hot tea still inside, were a regular party piece but it was his words that hurt most as he singled out several of us for particular criticism. Big Jack rarely blamed his team as a whole but would point the finger at individuals, including me. That was one day I hit back saying, if he'd made the signings I'd suggested earlier in the season, we would have stood a very good chance of getting promotion instead of being on the fringe. The boss was not amused. As far as Big Jack was concerned, his word was law and my opinions weren't wanted.

Apart from a 4-1 success over Hillsborough visitors Cambridge United two matches later, in which my partner in crime McCulloch netted a hat trick, it was all downhill from there. Four successive defeats, including a 1-0 reverse to champions West Ham in our final match, left us in tenth spot with 42 points from our 42 games. I was gutted that we finished so poorly after promising so much. In those crucial last dozen matches, we managed just two victories and six points, slipping from the third promotion spot to mid-table.

Donny Rovers, my first professional team and still dear to my heart. I'm third left on back row with assistant boss John Quigley (back, left), who christened me 'Terry', room mates Brendan O'Callaghan (back, fifth left) and Alan Murray (middle, third left), manager Stan Anderson (back right) and Peter Kitchen (middle, fifth left)

With Cloughie at Forest in 1976 – a Second Division side with a surprising sprinkling of future European Cup winners including a young Martin O'Neill, Viv 'spider' Anderson and the great John Robertson. I'm first left on front row

© Press Association

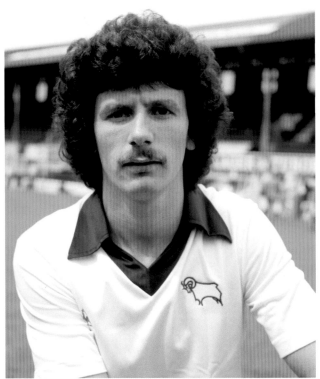

Not what the Doc ordered! I improved my cards with Tommy Docherty's Derby but not my football
© Press Association

Saints debut against Norwich City at Carrow Road

Scoring the League Cup semi final winner for Saints against Leeds – the celebration wasn't bad either

Measuring up well with my great pal, England's finest Alan Ball

Above and below – striding out with Saints for my one and only
Wembley date and skinning Forest's Frank Clark in the same match

On the Wednesday bench for my debut at Watford with
coach Ian St John and boss Big Jack
© Steve Ellis

Defenders back in the
day! Oldham's Kenny
Clements gets to grips
with me at Wednesday
© Steve Ellis

On me head son!
Scoring against Grimsby
to win £100 off Big Jack
© Steve Ellis

Singing The Blues.
I recorded the classic
song at Hull and
it is still played at
Hillsborough today
© Steve Ellis

Celebrations above and below – saluting the Hillsborough faithful and
enjoying the moment in a 2-1 win against Blackburn at Ewood Park
© Steve Ellis

Spot on against Wrexham at Hillsborough. In the background is
former Wales and Liverpool defender Joey Jones
© Steve Ellis

Tyke that! On target for the Owls against Barnsley

Going up! Jubilant Owls dressing room after the Carlisle match
© Steve Ellis

Receiving my Third Division Golden Boot award alongside my former Saints
colleague Phil Boyer (left) and QPR's Clive Allen

Flashpoint with Simon Stainrod at Oldham. The FA closed Hillsborough as a result of his acting. I got my revenge by scoring in the return against the Latics
© Steve Ellis

Shaping to score against one of my former clubs, Derby, for Wednesday. Rams defenders are Steve Powell and Roy McFarland
© Steve Ellis

I was Wednesday's free kick specialist before Big Jack came up with a bizarre Plan B
© Steve Ellis

A word in the ear of Owls colleague Ian Porterfield, who
became my boss at Bramall Lane
© Steve Ellis

In full flight – but my dribbling skills made me a target for the steel studs
© Steve Ellis

Two TCs in Sheffield! Warming up for Wednesday against Blades
legend Tony Currie, then with QPR
© Steve Ellis

Trying to look on the bright side of a 0-0 draw with Derby
with Monty Python's Michael Palin
© Steve Ellis

Talking myself into trouble with football's Old Bill
© Steve Ellis

WELCOME "EVERTON" THE C

We are the champions. Howard Kendall's Everton were by far
the best team I played for

In action for Everton
in the FA Cup semi
final against Saints.
We won 1-0
© Press Association

Part of the C crowd at
Huddersfield Town

Up the creek in Greece with former Manchester City star Gary Owen

Dressed to thrill
with partner
Lynne

I'm now a proud
parent to Tom
and Jock

Had Big Jack bolstered our numbers as well as our quality that would have helped us during the crucial run in. I've got no doubt the money was available if he had wanted to take the plunge.

Without being quite as prolific as the previous season, I finished as Wednesday's second top scorer playing mostly out wide with a respectable 11 in league and cup as McCulloch led the way with 18. It wasn't too difficult to work out our problem. We were excellent at home where we won 14 and lost just three but feeling blue on our travels where we had exactly the opposite record. There was plenty for us to chew over during the summer because we all knew this was one opportunity that slipped our grasp. Consolation for Wednesday fans was that the Blades, just a season after the Boxing Day massacre and now with former 1966 World Cup hero Martin Peters in charge, completed their nosedive into Division Four with a dramatic 1-0 home defeat by Walsall when they fell to a penalty in the last few minutes of the season

I was already in mixed books at Hillsborough not least as my column in the *Green 'Un*, Sheffield's Saturday night sports paper, got me into additional hot water. In one article I wrote about the uncovered Kop, arguing it should have a roof on it. Most fans probably agreed but that didn't amuse the chairman Bert McGhee who complained I was putting him in a difficult position because fans would expect him to stomp up some cash. That's chairmen for you.

I was about to enter the last year of my contract at Hillsborough and told Big Jack I needed more money of my own. He didn't offer me a wage rise but, to my surprise, came up with a great compromise – tearing up my contract! That's just what happened although there was no danger of me leaving Wednesday. Jack knew Swedish club Atvidabergs were interested in taking some English players and said I could play for them for a couple of months in the summer. It wasn't a loan as such so Wednesday cancelled my contract – whilst agreeing still to pay me and writing into the deal with

Atvidabergs that I would be returning to Sheffield for the new season.

Most of the Swedish sides were amateur although Malmo had emphasised the defensive quality of football there by getting through to the 1979 European Cup final against Forest – the game in which £1m man, Trevor Francis, stooped to head the only goal. Going to a country I'd never experienced before didn't worry me and, as it turned out, communication on all levels was absolutely great. The Swedes all spoke very good English and made me feel welcome. They even read the press reports of our games to me; the mostly good and occasionally not-so-good. I was on top of my game and enjoyed the chance to play up front in my nine games in Sweden. The social life, too, was fantastic.

I went out there with my wife and we lived in a bungalow leant to us by the club. But that didn't stop me from getting to know the Swedish ladies. I can see where former England manager Sven-Goran Erikkson gets it from because the women were the best looking I've seen in my whole life. I enjoyed meeting them in the cafe-style bars and night clubs and went back home to Sheffield with plenty of good memories! I also met up with my good mate Frank Worthington for an hour or two as he was with another Swedish club and the two sides went to the same cafe on their way to their respective matches. 'Elvis', as he is known, is a fantastic bloke and was definitely my kind of player – unbelievably talented and the type fans loved watching. His famous bicycle kick for Bolton Wanderers against Ipswich Town was one of the best goals I've ever seen – bettered only by George Best's incredible dribble for San Jose Earthquakes.

American football also interested me and moving to play in the States was one of the possibilities I was thinking over as I approached the last year of my contract with Wednesday. I didn't want to be one of those players who left it too late to go to the MLS and failed to produce their best form. America never happened and was just part of much speculation flying around about where I'd end up as it was now common knowledge Big Jack and I weren't seeing eye-to-eye. But all I was really interested in was trying to play my part to get Wednesday promoted and back where I felt they belonged – the First Division.

Jack pulled off a coup in the summer by landing Gary Bannister, who made a modest start to his goal poaching career at Coventry City and Detroit Express but was to become a big hit with Wednesday and QPR, netting more than 50 goals for both. That gave us more options to feed off either Andy McCulloch or John Pearson as our target man. It wasn't such great news for me, however, as I was used more often as an orthodox winger, reducing my own goal potential.

It also meant fewer opportunities for one of my closest friends at Wednesday Ian 'Spider' Mellor, who had written his name into folklore with that fantastic opening goal in the Boxing Day massacre. He was a Jack Charlton signing but that didn't stop him from getting some real abuse from the boss. There'd be about 1,500 fans watching training sessions at Middlewood Road and on one occasion Ian took a corner and shanked it straight behind the goal. Jack laced into him ranting and raving and insisting he took it again. As you can imagine, the lad was nervous and repeated his mistake by miskicking into the arms of the spectators. That prompted Jack to march over and say: "Look, this is how to take a corner." I don't think it even reached the first man!

Ian, whose son Neil was a big hit on loan with Wednesday in the 2010-11 season, is one of the blokes I still see from that era and has good reason to remember me. One day he asked me to come round to his house in Chapeltown to pick him up. I parked my car on the driveway and knocked on the door. A woman held it open as I brushed past her and headed for the settee. I had switched on the TV when the woman came into the lounge with a shocked look on her face. "Heh, you, what are you doing?" she said.

"Where's Spider?" I asked.

"He lives next door!" she replied.

Still makes me laugh when I think about it now. Funnier still was that the woman and her husband, who was also there at the time, were both very keen Sheffield United fans. It must have been bad enough having one of the Boxing Day scorers living next door without the Wednesday guy who'd done most to torment them barging into their house and making himself at home. The good thing was they were a lovely couple and saw the comical side of the incident.

Another story Ian likes telling is when a group of Wednesday lads, including Brian Hornsby, Jeff Johnson and Mick Pickering and himself, went into an Indian restaurant for a meal early one evening after a match. In I came, not thinking as usual, and said to the young Indian waiter very slowly and with my hand to my mouth acting out the words: "Where is the telephone?" He then answered in the broadest Yorkshire accent you've ever heard in your life as the other lads fell about laughing.

The 1981-82 season started with plenty of optimism, particularly as the boss had also splashed out £130,000 on a young midfielder from Everton called Gary Megson to strengthen us in another important area. It even looked as if we'd cured our travel sickness too as we won at Blackburn Rovers on opening day with my season getting off to a good start with the only goal. This kicked us off with three points as the 1981-82 campaign saw a change in the points system. The best was yet to come as we then went to one of the other fancied sides, Pleatie's Luton Town, and gave them a 3-0 thumping at Kenilworth Road. For some reason, I always seemed to do well against the Hatters and that was no exception. Although I didn't score, I was involved in all three goals – going on a 60-yard run for Andy McCulloch's first, providing the corner for Gary Megson to make it 2-0, then laying on a third for Bannister. The press were full of Wednesday and Terry Curran. TV cameras were there, too, to see us turn on a very impressive display. Jack was thrilled to pieces and uttered words he probably wished he'd have kept to himself when we fell out a few months later. "Terry is the most exciting player in the Football League at the moment," he said. "He has got the right qualities to play for his country. These days there are so many systems around that you need someone with individual ability to unlock them – Terry Curran can do that."

Two visitors were safely dispatched to make it four wins out of four with the bookies taking notice by quoting us as 3-1 favourites to lift the title. It wasn't until a 1-1 draw at the Baseball Ground in our fifth game that Derby County became the first team to score against us. Despite opening up an early four-point lead, I had no doubt where we needed to strengthen and lost Brownie points with Jack by telling him so. I said that Wednesday would walk promotion if we invested in a quality goalkeeper, centre half and striker. Jack didn't agree and was none too happy with me for poking my nose in. It was no surprise to me that soon after Jack and I were Hillsborough history, his successor Howard Wilkinson brought in Martin Hodge between the sticks, fellow former Evertonian Mickey Lyons as his blockbuster defender and Imre Varadi up front and took the team up. Enough said.

Despite suffering our first defeat at Barnsley, we were still top of the table at the end of September after I had a very mixed Saturday at Grimsby Town. I put us into the lead before being the victim of a very strong sliding tackle from a Mariners defender just before half time. He caught me on my right leg just below the knee and immediately the wound began gushing blood. I had eight stitches and was still on the physio's table when coach Tony Toms came in and asked me whether I could go back on the field. The former SAS man clearly had no time for softies!

In the meantime old foes returned to haunt us and check our early season charge. Those Welsh dragons from Wrexham again breathed their fire, beating us by three clear goals on our own patch. Then came a flying visit from my old 'mate'

Simon Stainrod, by now plying his trade with QPR. However many points he scored for diving, the bloke could certainly play a bit too, as he showed by scoring a mesmerising hat trick inside a five-minute spell just before half time as Rangers whipped us 3-1 at Hillsborough. I thought he was supposed to be a Wednesday fan! To be fair, he eventually did play for the Owls and started shooting in the right direction but that, fortunately perhaps, was after I was long gone. We then slipped to sixth as we lost 2-1 at Stamford Bridge against Chelsea on December 5 and the icy blast meant we didn't play again in the league until January 16 when Blackburn grabbed a 2-2 draw at Hillsborough.

I'd been having a fair amount of success in our Second Division days taking the direct free kicks until one night at St James' Park where I had two or three opportunities to have a go at goal during a midweek match at Newcastle but saw my efforts either blocked by the wall or sail high over the bar. It was a frustrating night generally as, despite creating several opportunities, we trudged off the pitch having lost 1-0. I may have been frustrated but Big Jack went crazy – with me as the main target. "You aren't going to be taking any of our free kicks again," he stormed. Seemed like an over-reaction to me as you can never guarantee being successful from free kicks, but the manager was clearly determined to make his point.

Next day he turned up on the training ground looking more like a holidaymaker in Skeggy than a top rate football manager and told us with boyish enthusiasm that he'd thought of a unique set piece. None of us had a clue what was going to happen next especially as Jack's tracksuit bottoms were about three-quarters up his legs and he was wearing one sports sock and another he'd had with his suit the previous evening.

"This is what we're going to do with our free kicks from now on," he said, sounding like a headmaster as most of us were still trying to hold back fits of laughter at his appearance. To our surprise, he pointed at Gary Megson to come forward – although he was a fair striker of the ball, to be honest. Next he beckoned to Gary Bannister and myself and explained we should stand just in front of the defensive wall. We would run bent over back towards Megs, who'd aim his shot against one of our backs from where it would deflect into the back of the net. Got it? I couldn't stop myself laughing at such a crazy plan but Big Jack was in no mood for a joke. "Get yourself off the pitch, Terry, and go and have a shower," he shouted. I was more than happy to be out of the firing line but no shower could be as interesting as seeing Big Jack's free kick in action. Standing at the side of the pitch, I couldn't believe my eyes as the manager lumbered up to the ball. He was an uncompromising centre half but ability-wise on the training ground made Lawrie McMenemy look like Maradona. However, on this occasion, he swung a lazy boot and watched with great pride as his shot hit Bano on the back and somehow ended up in the net. Big Jack stood there beaming as the rest of the lads doubled up in laughter.

We knew we would be testing out the masterplan for real at Cardiff City on the Saturday. Megs took aim and, when the ball was blocked by our own defensive wall, visiting fans could hardly believe what they had just seen. Fortunately, they were able to see the funny side as went home with a 2-0 victory.

In the matches that followed, Megs always came up with an excuse for not giving Big Jack's free kick another try. "I didn't think it was on, boss, in that situation," he'd say and Jack walked away reasonably satisfied. I think managers sometimes look to create a name for themselves by being the first to think of a free kick or corner move, wanting to take the credit for being particularly clever. It makes me laugh when a free kick goal is scored during a game on TV and the commentator says "and that was a move straight from the training ground . . ." In all probability it has been tried and failed endless times before it finally works. My policy was to keep the game simple: if I got a free kick within 25 or 30 yards of goal and thought the shot was on, I'd have a go. You can blind everyone with science but the aim of the game is still to get the ball between the sticks!

Big Jack definitely had his qualities but sometimes it seemed we were being managed by Ricky Tomlinson, the comedy actor who did such a good take off of an England manager. Jack often wrote his team on a cigarette packet – a habit that definitely reminds me of Ricky's character Mike Bassett – and another classic touch was his chronic problems remembering names. He had Jeff King and Andy McCulloch staying at his house while both were trying to find permanent accommodation after signing for Wednesday – trust Big Jack to think of every possible way of squeezing out a few more pennies. For ages he referred to his new signings as Andy King – the name of the Luton and Everton midfielder – and Jeff McCulloch, a name from his own imagination. Let's put it this way: if Jack knew your name he was having a particularly good day!

We weren't quite in the Don Revie class of producing near books on the tactics of our opposition but always sent a scout to report on our next opponents so the boss could decide how to combat them. The problem was in the translation. The report was written in longhand on a piece of paper and it was good fun hearing Big Jack trying to read it out. He'd shake his head every few sentences and pass it on to his assistant Maurice Setters, my first boss from Donny, to see if he could make head or tail of it. Setters was usually none the wiser and eventually both would admit defeat.

There was also an incident in the club gymnasium as we were preparing for a match against Norwich City that almost got out of hand. I'd been playing in my favourite position up front but Big Jack suddenly barked out that I'd be on the right wing against the Canaries.

"No, I won't – if you want a right winger, pick Gordon Owen," I replied.

"I am telling you – you are playing on the right," said Jack getting angrier and angrier. He'd been about 50 yards away at the beginning of the argument and was now closing in on me with every second. When he got near enough he took a swing at me. Had he connected, he'd have probably knocked me through the gymnasium wall. I ducked out of his way and grabbed him around the midriff as fellow players gathered to pull the two of us apart to ensure it didn't get a whole lot worse. The results of the fracas were much better for Big Jack than for me. He picked Owen and we won 3-2 before telling the press I'd been guilty of a 'couldn't care less' attitude. I put in a written transfer request reminding Big Jack that my deal was up at the end of the season and I could walk away then. The media, as you can imagine, lapped it up eagerly. To be honest, I was completely out of order throughout the whole episode.

Another personal gripe was Big Jack singling me out for criticism in his after match interviews. It happened once too often after we'd been beaten 2-1 at Hillsborough by Chelsea. It seemed the manager was blaming me whenever the team lost yet praising everyone else when we were successful and it was getting on my nerves. I knew I wasn't having the same spectacular influence – or scoring as many goals – as I had in my first two seasons at Wednesday, but I put some of that down to the close marking I was attracting. Opponents often doubled up on me, making it very difficult to find the space I was used to, but opening up more room for other Wednesday players to profit. What I didn't accept was Jack's public comment that I didn't care. Nobody took their football more seriously than I did – the reason I got into trouble was I cared too much rather than too little. I showed him what I could do by netting a hat trick against Sheffield United Reserves but, with Jack insisting on an apology that was never going to come, I handed in a transfer request as I was frustrated at being frozen out for no good reason.

There were endless column inches in the local and national press throughout the season speculating on the latest state of my up and down relationship with Jack and suggesting I'd be on my bike come May. Even telling them I was keeping my mouth shut and head down before deciding my future when the football was over didn't stop them. One of the more interesting stories linked me with a move to West German club Schalke 04, who'd just won the Second Division title and were preparing for life back in the Bundesliga, but nothing came of it. There was even talk of interest from Australian sides Sydney FC and Newcastle.

We remained hit and miss for the first couple of months of the New Year before a good run suddenly shot us back into real promotion contention. Bannister got himself a couple of crucial goals as first we began to ease the trauma of our previous visit to Boundary Park by thrashing Oldham Athletic 3-0 and then cashed in at Hillsborough by beating Leicester City 2-0. We then made it three out of three by beating Orient at home by the same scoreline.

QPR again stopped us in our tracks before we defeated Shrewsbury, Newcastle and Cambridge to have Wednesday fans in buoyant mood. I still can hardly believe it when I look back on the league table with just five matches left. There we were in third spot six points clear of our nearest challengers Rotherham United with Norwich City, who eventually pipped us, a mind boggling nine points back with one game in hand. What went wrong for us in the next four matches, I still don't fully know – but it will haunt me forever. My dream of playing for Wednesday in the First Division disappeared in smoke in front of my eyes.

It all started with a 4-0 thrashing at Watford, fast becoming one of my bogey grounds, followed by having to settle for a point from both Chelsea and Rotherham United. The Canaries were now one point ahead of us after a vital run of four wins on the bounce, but we still had promotion in our own hands as Norwich were due at Hillsborough on the last day. So we went to Bolton for our penultimate match with hopes still high and half an eye on Norwich's game at Orient.

That wasn't my most prolific goalscoring season by a long

shot as I only scored three in the league and none at all at Hillsborough. But I got on the scoresheet in the first half at Burnden Park and we reached the interval at 1-1. The next 45 minutes were a disaster, however, as Bolton scored twice more to defeat us 3-1 and the worst of all news came through from Brisbane Road – Norwich had won and were promoted. We were out of the hunt even before the last match as champions Luton Town and Watford had already booked their tickets to the top flight. The fact we defeated Norwich 2-1 in what was by then a meaningless finale at Hillsborough made our collapse all the more frustrating. We should have been sipping champagne but instead didn't know where to put ourselves.

My third and last season at Hillsborough was at an end and I consoled myself by meeting up with another maverick – this time at The Crucible. I spent three strange days with one of the sport's most amazing characters, Alex 'Hurricane' Higgins, during the 1982 world championships for which he is most fondly remembered. I was just an average snooker fan but Higgins was the player who fascinated me most. He'd gate crashed his way to a world title in 1972 when nobody had ever heard of him and subsequently set the game alight by playing at a speed nobody had seen before. He was snooker's version of George Best; almost as compulsive a magnet for the ladies as the great man, Alex was also a flawed genius who would have won far more had he conquered his demons.

When I met up with him in Josephine's, he was on his way to that very memorable second world title when, after famously defeating the comparatively staid Canadian Cliff Thorburn, he instinctively called for his wife and daughter and held the young girl with tears of raw emotion filling his eyes. Sadly it was nearly all downhill from there for the Hurricane who in later years was ravaged by throat cancer and was a pitiful sight long before his sad, lonely death in July 2010. I spent three virtually full days with him and the signs of his pain to come were all there. The bloke was clearly a bag of nerves, not eating anything but instead popping pills and drinking alcohol. If you'd been in his hotel room during that championship, you would never have guessed he was a top sportsman – the place was literally full of medication and booze.

Among several things we shared in common was our love of gambling and unpredictability. I remember him now telling me he was going to win that tournament and he was going to put £5,000 on himself at the bookies. I was so impressed with his confidence I agreed to wager £2,500. Yet when we got there, we both stuck our cash on one of his main rivals Steve Davis. As many of you will remember, Higgins then went on to lift the title for the second time and share that emotional moment with his young daughter. I left the Crucible poorer financially, but with some precious memories of an amazing talent.

I think he eventually suffered because he couldn't control his nerves and concentrate fully on the individual shots that are the difference between winning and losing when sport is played at such a high level. I remain very grateful for the chance to meet the Hurricane and also enjoyed going to Maine Road with him one night. Naturally, I saw something of myself in him. Both of us may have under sold ourselves talent-wise, but I'd like to think we both entertained and left behind more than our fair share of memories.

I'd come to the end of my three-year deal at Wednesday and still expected to sign another one. I was playing for the football club I idolised and living in a city I loved – even though my domestic life was complicated, I was in no rush to move on. Playing-wise I hadn't been as spectacularly successful since my first full season but I was still a big hero with Wednesday fans and thought I'd played a major role in taking us to the very verge of the First Division. I had personal differences with Jack but felt confident he would put these aside and offer me a very good deal in the best interests of Sheffield Wednesday. I wanted £500 a week and an £11,000 tax free payment to completely pay off my mortgage but Jack, whilst happy to match my figures, refused to make the payment tax free.

I was furious with Jack and my uncertain future quickly alerted other clubs. But the next approach really blew my head off. A friend of Reg Brealey, chairman of our bitter rivals Sheffield United, phoned to ask whether I'd switch across the city to Bramall Lane. It took me just a split second to reply and the answer was an emphatic 'no'. But suddenly an offer of £50,000 over two years was made and, for the only time in my career, I became seduced by the money. I told Brealey at his house in Spalding I would sign for United but, as the two clubs failed to agree a fee, it went to a tense tribunal held at the Royal Victoria Hotel. Jack suddenly offered me the tax free payment after all – but it was too late.

The tribunal caused me very mixed emotions. I knew I'd come out a winner in one way as I was sure to be better off financially but also felt horrible because I knew in my heart I was letting down the club I supported as man and boy. Jack thought he'd make a fair profit on the £100,000 Wednesday paid out and demanded £250,000. United offered £50,000. The local media lapped up the drama – two bitter rivals slugging it out over a temperamental and talented player with me as piggy in the middle. Big Jack dropped a bombshell during the evidence that First Division Everton had made a £500,000 offer for me – something I knew absolutely nothing about. He probably thought that mentioning such a massive club was interested would influence the officials into raising the final fee. Brealey gave me a talking to about what I should say, but I already knew how to play it. I was so fed up with Jack I was determined to make things as hard as possible for him. I told the tribunal I'd signed for Wednesday for £100,000 and given them three good years, so the fee now should be similar. I argued that I couldn't possibly have been worth the £500,000 Everton offered because my wages at Wednesday weren't in that league.

Big Jack was shocked when the figure was fixed at £100,000

– the look on his face betrayed his true feelings. He came up to me and said he hoped I got everything I deserved. The boss did his best to convince the press he was happy to see me leave, but we both knew the truth. It was a sad, sad way to leave Sheffield Wednesday and didn't do either of us any favours. I console myself today with the thought I had many more good times than bad with both Wednesday and Big Jack and am pleased there are no hard feelings between us. We last met up for our latest Boxing Day massacre reunion in February 2012.

With the most controversial of deals rapped up, I took a phone call from Newcastle United manager Arthur Cox. There he was offering me the opportunity to go to St James Park, one of the undoubted hot spots of football, to play in a forward line of Chris Waddle down the left, Kevin Keegan and Peter Beardsley in the middle and myself on the right. Compare this with the prospect of playing for a Third Division club whose fans regarded me as public enemy number one. Yet I felt there was no going back on the Blades deal. After the Oldham affair, my public fallings out with Jack and a very heated tribunal, I daren't go back on what had been agreed.

Of all the decisions I have made in my whole life moving from Wednesday to their deadly rivals was without doubt the craziest of the lot. Talk about being the wrong person in the wrong place at the wrong time – there are mistakes and mistakes but joining Sheffield United was a whopper by any standards. Getting my own back at Big Jack for not offering the terms I was looking for at Wednesday was a terrible reason to go to Bramall Lane. But I can't come up with a better one now because that was the truth. My only other excuse was my love of the Sheffield night life. I can only apologise once again to both sets of fans for what I did. The only part I can look back on with pride is that I stuck to my word. When Big Jack came calling in that Leeds night club, I told him I'd sign for Wednesday and I did even though Saints weren't happy about it; likewise I kept my promise to the Blades chairman even though I could have backed out right at the end.

Brealey obviously thought he'd won some local prestige by landing Wednesday's best known player and would boost Blades manager Ian Porterfield's chances of gaining a second successive promotion after winning the Fourth Division title in some style the previous season. But he was also being naïve. It has never been easy for anyone to move from Wednesday to United or vice versa – the statisticians tell me only 26 players have ever pulled on both red and blue in Sheffield. But, for a fans' favourite with Wednesday in his blood, it was totally impossible. I'd wasted no chance to rub United's noses in it whilst at Hillsborough, a fact true Unitedites weren't going to forget in a hurry. I don't blame them to be honest. I let both sets of fans down and deserved most of the stick I got.

Opinions differ on how well I played at Bramall Lane. I thought I did quite well during most of my 33 games – but, whatever your opinion, I know I always gave 100 per cent. I could never play football any other way – whether in a cup final or a village match. I could understand getting stick from the fans, particularly when things weren't going our way. I remember one midweek match against Reading at Bramall Lane where I came in for a lot of abuse. It was a 7.30pm kick off and when I saw it was 9pm on the stadium clock I knew there were probably only about ten more minutes to go with the scores level at 1-1. I tried everything possible to get us the winning goal. True, I wasn't passing to anyone but that was because I was so desperate to score. I tried to beat every Tom, Dick and Harry but it just wasn't to be. We did everything but win that night. Afterwards I went to Josephine's to wind down and was confronted by an angry Blades fan just outside the door. "Get back to Wednesday, Curran, you never tried a leg tonight," he said. Little did he know but I'd put £500 on us to win at evens so, even apart from professional pride, I couldn't have been any keener for us to succeed.

Thinking I was onto a good thing living and socialising in Sheffield proved a big mistake. Moving to United meant I had to be a whole lot more careful where I was seen out as I now had two sets of angry Sheffield fans on my case. One incident came when I was having what I hoped would be a quiet meal in an Italian restaurant. Suddenly one of the fellow guests came up to me and starting shouting the odds, telling me exactly what he thought of a Wednesdayite coming to play at the Lane. He wanted to fight whilst I just wanted to get out. Incidents like that played a part in my eventual decision to turn my back on football when my playing days were over. I never got used to it and didn't like it. I was as likely as any player to have a chat with supporters – and it's really sad so much of that has gone out of the game – but I didn't go out on the town to fight.

The Blades' players themselves were mixed; some were fine with me, others not so good. Two of the lads I got on best with were two of the strongest Unitedites – Tony Kenworthy, always a mate despite our running battle a couple of years before, and John McPhail, the other guy who'd threatened to break my leg at Hillsborough. It was a matter of letting bygones be bygones and getting to know each other better. I went out on the town with both of them and we got on great. Kenworthy was actually a Leeds United fan and McPhail a rugged Scot but their commitment to the Blades was total. They understood me and I understood them; I've got total respect for anyone true to his club, that's what it should be all about. They knew I was a Wednesdayite at heart and took the mickey out of me without it ever getting nasty.

I was also mates with Alan Young, a likeable Scottish striker who knew what it was like to move down the leagues having played in the top flight with Leicester City and joined the Blades around the same time as me. He reckons now I invited myself to stay at his house and didn't leave for months but I reckon he must have lost something in translation. He also says the Blades needed two balls that season – one for the rest of the lads whilst I kept the real one to myself. Or was Youngie just too slow to find any space? Anyway, that's all good football banter and we're still friends.

I didn't really get on with Blades striker Keith Edwards, who had scored 35 goals the previous season and went on to become a near legend at Bramall Lane. It wasn't a case of anything nasty; we were just two different personalities. He was a selfish kind of striker in the best sense of the word. Like Gary Lineker, it never crossed his mind to pass when the goal was in sight and that is usually the mark of a very good goalscorer. He didn't like the idea of a Wednesdayite coming to the club and possibly stealing some of his thunder. There was never really any danger of me doing so however.

The training was awful as Blades coach Jim Dixon, a former marathon runner, made us run, run and run. We did five-mile hikes up hills as if preparing for marathons ourselves rather than football matches. You can imagine how much good that did to my battered limbs. There was rarely any ball work which matched our style as it spent most of Saturday afternoon flying over my head anyway. I could never understand Edwards spending lots of time taking corners. Surely he would have been better off in the penalty area doing what he did best? The other problem I had at United was I never got the feeling Porterfield really wanted me there. I was very much the chairman's signing and that didn't make things easy for either manager or player.

It probably didn't help my Bramall Lane experience that I was going through difficult times in my personal life. I'd separated from my wife Kim, telling her that I needed some space – to go out and bed some more women, of course. My next major relationship had shades of the Human League, the Sheffield-based group of new romantics who were regulars in the charts at the time. Dishy Lorraine really was 'working as a waitress in a cocktail bar' as their famous song went. She was on the staff at Josephine's and I took to her straightaway. I was still a regular there so we could meet her on the job and soon started going out.

I didn't wear a wedding ring and Lorraine had no idea

about Kim. It was only when we hadn't seen each other for a couple of weeks that she found out. Somehow she got hold of my home telephone number and Kim answered. I then told her straight that I had been married and was separated and Lorraine took it well. Things started to develop between us and I soon moved from my digs into Lorraine's house in Dover Road. Everything was going well until one night when I played in a reserve match against Manchester United's second string at Bramall Lane. I was sat in the bath thinking a young lad called Paul McGrath, who was playing in defence for the Reds that night, was a great prospect when Kenworthy came up to me with a big smile all over his face. "I think you'd better go home mate," he beamed. "Your wife's at home!" That was news to him as he didn't know I even had one. I couldn't blame him because no one would have guessed I was wed the way I was with women when we were out together! But it was news to me also as Kim and I weren't living together anymore – shit, Kim must be at Lorraine's!

I drove home in panic not knowing what on earth to expect when I got to the front door. Running into Liverpool hard man Tommy Smith or Leeds United's Norman 'bite your legs' Hunter was frightening, but nothing compared with both the women in your life being in the same place at the same time! I opened the door in terror as Lorraine passed me on the way out shouting "you need to sort this mess out!" before leaving to stay the night with a nearby friend. Kim and her mum were inside. Somehow they'd found out about me being shacked up with another woman and were spitting feathers. I had a good chat with Kim, telling her what she didn't want to hear – I wasn't going to go back to her. Of course, she was fed up but she took the news pretty well. Perhaps it was just the relief that she was at last getting the truth and the air was being cleared. So somehow I got out from what could have been a terrible situation without too much damage. When Lorraine returned home next day, I told her exactly what had happened and she was happy enough with my explanation to give our relationship another chance.

Considering my problems at home and on the field, news Everton wanted to take me on loan came as a huge lift. Porterfield asked what I thought and I said I'd love to go there. I got on reasonably well with Porterfield on a personal level but he didn't fight too hard to dissuade me. When you think about it, it was an odd thing for the Blades to do – they'd pulled off a local coup by signing Wednesday's most high profile player on a three-year deal and now, less than four months and just 14 games later, they were prepared to let me spend time at Goodison Park. I wasn't going to worry myself about that – I'd have gladly have walked all the way to Merseyside to play in the First Division again.

7

We Are the Champions!

"We were a terrific side in the making at Everton with a lot of youngish lads in the squad when in came TC from the Third Division like a breath of fresh air and gave everyone a big lift. Having played against him on several occasions, I already knew just how good TC was. Yes, he was a maverick and an entertainer, but he was a whole lot more than that – this guy could really play. He had skill and pace and was brave both physically and mentally. If you gave TC the ball, you knew he could look after it for you. Without doubt, he was a part of the great Everton success story that followed – and could have been a bigger part. When people like Cloughie and Jack Charlton say he could have played for England, I don't need to say any more. Guess that's partly why TC calls this book Regrets because he under achieved for his talent. There's no doubt he could have played in the Premier League today – full backs wouldn't have known what to do now they couldn't kick him up in the air all afternoon! He was head strong and single minded and that proved his undoing at Everton in the end but he was always my cup of tea, both on and off the field. TC has great personality and was a big hit with the lads socially. TC knows his football and is always enthusiastic – even when falling out with someone!"

Peter Reid, Everton (1982-89) and England

IT WAS written in the stars I'd eventually play for Everton Football Club. After all, they chased me for long enough! I've already said how Harry Catterick showed an interest in taking me to Goodison Park before I joined Forest from Donny Rovers. But I made no contact with the club back then because my mind was set on playing for Brian Clough. There was more flirting from the Toffees towards the end of my time at Hillsborough, although I was unaware of it at the time. Now one of the most famous clubs in the land had me on their radar yet again after I'd been at Bramall Lane for a few months.

Former playing legend, Howard Kendall, was the manager and in need of a lift. His team was struggling and he didn't have a whole lot of money in the pot to put it right – so he reached down into the Third Division to take me for a month. Joining Everton at long last at the beginning of December 1982 was a no-brainer for me. Kendall and Everton had what looked, on paper, to be one of the best squads in the country. There was no shortage of talent throughout the team with Gary Stevens and John Bailey in the full back positions, Mark Higgins and Kevin Ratcliffe in central defence, Steve McMahon, Kevin Richardson, Andy King and Kevin Sheedy – he of the left foot to die for – across the midfield and competition for places up front too. Scottish international Graeme Sharp was the leading goalscorer that season with Adrian Heath and David Johnson completing what was on paper a terrific strike force.

For some reason, however, it just wasn't gelling and, after a couple of high scoring home victories over Aston Villa 5-0 and Spurs 3-1, the Goodison Park fans were definitely getting restless. When I tell you only 16,001 turned out for the previous home match – a 0-0 draw against West Bromwich – you need to consider also that Everton were living in the shadows of their close and fierce rivals Liverpool. The glory days at the beginning of the 1970s with that fantastic midfield of Bally, Kendall and Colin Harvey and the goals of big Joe Royle were being fast forgotten as the Reds had long since emerged as the dominant force, not only locally, but nationally and in Europe too. I was, of course, well used to bitter rivalries – Forest and Derby, Saints and Pompey, Wednesday and United as well as the village spats between Fitzwilliam and Hemsworth. The point I'm making is that local rivalries are the same wherever you play. It's just the scale of the battleground that changes and the number of fans who show their allegiance and hatred.

Don't get me wrong, it's something players take on board. We may have bumped into Liverpool lads like Mark Lawrenson and Ronnie Whelan in the Merseyside bars, but on the field for 90 minutes it was full-on with both sets of players desperately keen to win bragging rights just as much as points. Just a month before I went there, more than 52,000 fans witnessed a slaughter that these days might have been enough alone to guarantee the manager's exit – a 5-0 home beating at the hands of Liverpool. That was the obvious lowlight of an eight-match winless run that had seen the lads nosedive into 15th place – the last three without a single goal to cheer – and what did the manager do? He took a winger on loan who had been in and out of the Sheffield United side. I fully realised how it may have looked to the fans. It had been more than 3 years since I'd played top flight football and, at 28, some skeptics will have wondered whether I was still the flying machine who once terrorised defences. Could I still do it at the top level?

The risk wasn't as great from my point of view. I was more than happy to swap the insults being thrown in my direction at Bramall Lane for a few doubters at Goodison Park. The chance to test myself at the highest level was just what I needed with my career in danger of drifting. Just walking into the training ground at Belfield gave me an idea how massive a club Everton was. It was the first and only club I went to with its own indoor gym and whose players had a meal together after training as attention was given to nutrition. All that was lacking were a few good results.

A month in a different setting was a great social opportunity too. Girlfriends always had to put up with a lot with me moving from one club to another but the chance of getting away temporarily was just about ideal. Fortunately, Lorraine wasn't the jealous, in-your-face type. She was a quiet girl who preferred an evening in front of the TV to going out and happily accepted my excuse that I'd be better off staying on Merseyside than commuting from Sheffield every day of the week. So I set up camp in a Holiday Inn and came back home after the match on a Saturday.

Compared with the hostile atmosphere between Everton and Liverpool generally, relationships were very cordial at the hotel where Reds striker David Hodgson was in a nearby room having signed from Middlesbrough. The look on his face said it all. He'd be in the lift coming down from his room with his wife and see me coming up with yet another girl on my arm. I told him to keep it quiet from his team mates and he always did. He seemed to think my lifestyle was quite funny. I was making friends with members of the Everton squad, notably 'Bales' Bailey and 'Inchy' Heath, but didn't want word of what was going on to get around. I was playing away from home and Lorraine was unlikely to find out – but, if you do socialise with team mates in such circumstances, there's always a chance their wives and girlfriends will let your other half know.

Footballers never have trouble picking up girls so that was good for a kick off. The other killer lines included being holed up in a nice hotel – that always adds a touch of excitement. Throw in dashing looks and personality and there were always plenty of women to pick from. Sales reps and managers stay there whilst working, then there are the hotel staff. My game plan was to go down to the bar in the evening and find a young lady to talk to. Then we'd share a drink or a meal and, more than likely, a bed for the night! It was one romp after another and a very good way of celebrating what also turned out to be a very good time for me on the pitch. I had no desire to hurt Lorraine – it was a case of what she didn't know couldn't upset her. There was no finer way to spend an evening – and a night – than chatting to a lovely looking woman. The majority were probably married but that didn't really matter to either of us. In fact it was probably a good thing. I didn't want to get involved whilst they were making the most of a chance to get away from their usual life with their husbands. It certainly made my month at Everton all the more memorable.

Back on the pitch, my Everton debut came on Saturday, December 4 in a boring 0-0 draw at home to Birmingham that offered little hint of the fireworks to come. Perhaps we should have known what to expect from a Brum side managed by Ron Saunders whose teams never gave much away. I was playing on the right flank and opposed that afternoon by a formidable tackler by the name of Pat Van Den Hauwe, later to become a team mate at Goodison Park. We had Adrian Heath alongside Sharpy up front as we drew a fourth successive blank in front of goal. Perhaps the most striking statistic of a less than memorable game was the attendance of just 13,707. I didn't get myself a goal or even make one but did enough to catch the eye of another maverick Everton hero, Duncan McKenzie, who wrote that he'd enjoyed seeing me give Van Den Hauwe the slip, then make a point of telling him I wished him better luck next time!

Stepping back up two divisions didn't worry me at all. Some reporters asked whether I was nervous starting again in the top flight with Everton. I told them very honestly that I wasn't. What could be better than playing for a massive football club in a fantastic stadium? I knew I belonged. I was often accused of being arrogant but I'd prefer to call it confidence as, from my days with Kinsley Boys onwards, I always knew I could play the game. Being on the top stage, alongside players who thought and acted so much quicker than in the Third Division, was ideal. That was always going to make me look a better player.

Proof came seven days later against a talented Ipswich Town, who were just outside the top six, at Portman Road. Although Bobby Robson was no longer in charge, the Town line up included many star players from the famous side he took to glory in both the FA Cup and the UEFA Cup. Between the sticks was Paul Cooper, a very good goalkeeper and kingpin at saving penalties; George Burley, Terry Butcher and

Russell Osman were in the back four, with Dutch maestro Franz Thijssen, John Walk, Stuart McCall and Eric Gates in a star quality midfield and Paul Mariner and Alan Brazil up front. Beat that little lot, you might say – and we did in some style. I had a very good game on the right, setting up goals for both Kevin Richardson and Kevin Sheedy in an excellent 2-0 victory that broke our goal drought and lifted us a couple of places up the table.

Our goalie during that spell was one Jim Arnold, who had to be the worst dressed player at the club. Brown was his favourite colour which was very appropriate because most of the time he looked crap! Flares were in but they wouldn't have been had the fashion experts seen our Jim wearing them. Talk about *Jim'll Fix It*, he was more like Jim'll Wreck It. Another of his crazy touches was a huge tie – so large you could have made a couple of pairs of trousers or even curtains out of the material. One day I did the decent thing, both for Jim and for mankind, by getting a knife and cutting it into a thousand different pieces before blaming it on Inchy. Poor Jim threatened to cut up my shoes when I came in for training on the Monday. But I was too smart for that and hid my stuff – an experienced footballer like me was well used to the type of pranks others played and ensured I stayed out of trouble. As you've probably guessed, Jim was also a great lad as well as a very capable keeper but had no chance once a certain Neville Southall, a new signing from Bury, became first choice. More, much more about the big man later.

Ipswich was just a taster for what was probably my finest hour and a half in an Everton shirt on the Saturday before Christmas. The fans hadn't quite got the message as only 14,982 turned out to see us face David Pleat's Luton Town who were fighting a relegation battle. Virtually everything went right for the lads that day. I celebrated my third game with my first Everton goal and set up two more for Inchy as we ran riot in a 5-0 victory. Blimey, even Bales got himself on the scoresheet – and we never heard the last of it! This is what really happened: Bales got the ball just inside the Hatters' half and launched a high punt forward that got caught in the slight wind and flew over Les Sealey, not the tallest of goalkeepers. Here is Bales' version: he spotted Sealey off his line, took aim and, hey presto, the ball was in the back of the net for Goal of the Century. He never tired of telling us about it over a few drinks. No, even that's not true. He never stopped telling us about that goal over a lot of drinks! That game was also very memorable for me. It was great to hear the Everton fans singing 'sign him up, sign him up' and 'let's have a whip round' and Kendall saying I'd helped his team turn the corner. If I thought the move to Goodison Park would be easy, however, I was in for a big shock.

It was a very hectic month. I played all seven games in a whirlwind 27-day spell, including the last four inside a week. Squad rotation wasn't an issue as just 13 players took part in that grueling festive period. I don't think Premier League sides these days would ever agree to such a schedule and would use almost all of their 25-man squads to cope with anything similar. But the game wasn't as quick in those days, nor were the pitches anything like the billiard tables you see now. The muddy, bobbly surfaces helped to slow the game down and give us some respite.

Our next match was on the Monday, two days after Christmas, enabling the lads to celebrate Christmas Day itself with our families. I went back to Sheffield to share some time with Lorraine and gave her a heavily edited version of how much fun I was having on Merseyside. We then went into training on Boxing Day before travelling to Stoke and staying overnight in the Potteries. Everything was done to ensure there was little chance of the mood of celebration getting out of hand but it didn't help us too much the next afternoon as we went down to a single goal by England winger Mark Chamberlain. The formidable defensive barrier of Dave Watson and George Berry then helped to keep that lead intact. Two other notable names in the Stoke side were Sammy McIlroy and Mickey

Thomas, both former Manchester United stars.

There was no time for us to dwell on that disappointment because just 24 hours later we were back at Goodison Park to entertain Cloughie's Forest. This was the first time I'd faced my former boss since being on the losing side with Saints at Wembley and, although Forest were much changed after their double European Cup triumph, they travelled to Merseyside in an impressive second position. There was only one team in it that day, however, and it wasn't Cloughie's. Sharpy helped himself to a couple of first half goals and Steve McMahon also got himself on the scoresheet. Strangely enough, I never got the impression Kendall really fancied the combative midfielder who was in and out of the side but he certainly became a big name when he made a controversial move to Liverpool and enjoyed a lot of success there.

Midfielder Steve Hodge got one back for Forest but it wasn't enough to prevent them going down 3-1. With a strange sense of irony, I was in direct opposition to Bryn Gunn, the lad I'd made my Forest debut with. I had the better of Gunn that afternoon, enough for Cloughie to have a chat with me as I was leaving the pitch and ask whether I fancied a return to Trentside. I told him 'yes' because I definitely wanted to be back full time in the top flight. A permanent move to Goodison Park had obviously crossed my mind, but going to another First Division club – including being reunited with the great man at Forest – also appealed. As it turned out, I heard no more from Forest and I was shuffled back a little reluctantly to Bramall Lane after appearing in two more festive matches – a 2-2 draw against West Brom at The Hawthorns in which I gave England defender Derek Statham quite a chasing to bring in the New Year and a 2-1 defeat at Spurs two days later.

It had been a whirlwind month both on the field and in the hotel bedroom and hard but enjoyable work all round. The disappointing thing when I returned to Sheffield was that my success on Merseyside had the opposite effect to the one I was looking for. Instead of guaranteeing me a move to Everton or

Forest, it merely increased Brealey's determination to keep hold of me. My profile was raised by our FA Cup clashes with First Division Stoke City. We drew 0-0 at Bramall Lane and there was a rumour United were going to pull me out of the midweek replay as Everton tried to complete a deal. They wanted to sign me permanently and were offering to extend Trevor Ross's loan spell at Bramall Lane. But it all fell through and the replay at the Victoria Ground muddied the waters still further. We went out of the Cup 3-2 that night but I had an evening when virtually everything I touched turned to gold. I may not have got myself on the scoresheet but set up a couple for Keith Edwards and generally had one of my very best games. Very good timing as Everton, Arsenal and Manchester United all had scouts watching.

There then followed a scramble for my services by four First Division clubs – resulting in one of the biggest let downs of my whole career. First to make a move were Everton, who agreed a £100,000 fee with the Blades. Cloughie was as good as his word and was also prepared to pay that figure but the real eye-opener was Manchester United coming calling. Ron Atkinson was the Old Trafford manager but the approach came from a journalist called Norman Winn who phoned up and asked whether I'd be interested in joining United. What do you think? They were the most famous club in the land, the one I'd idolised since I was a schoolboy. You bet I was interested. Things then got complicated when Don Howe at Arsenal declared his hand. Brealey suddenly realised he was onto a good thing and upped my price from £100,000 to £500,000. Here I was, a one-time skinny lad from a mining village, being courted by four of the most famous teams in the world. I'd have gladly walked all the way to Goodison Park, Highbury, the City Ground and, particularly, Old Trafford to play for any one of them.

The way the United interest was handled gutted me and was something I could never forgive Porterfield for. Manchester set a deadline for a deal to be completed whilst

Porterfield and the chairman played for time. Basically unless I signed by 1pm on a particular Saturday they would turn their attentions elsewhere. The deadline passed with no deal in sight and United were as good as their word as they snapped up Scottish winger Arthur Graham instead.

This has got to be one of my greatest regrets in football. Although Sheffield Wednesday will always be my club, United have also had a place in my heart from my youth. They were just beginning to emerge from a relatively barren period – and I could have been a part of it if Porterfield and co hadn't been so stubborn. It still annoys me when I think about it now that I missed out on the chance of being at United when Sir Alex Ferguson began his glorious Old Trafford revolution. As so often, the carrot I'd been waiting for all my career was dangled in front of me, then whipped away almost immediately.

It was a similar story with Arsenal. They got fed up with the wait and turned to Brian Marwood, a striker from Hull City. Everton were put off by the much higher fee and Cloughie was understandably cautious about splashing the cash having seen his £1m on Justin Fashanu backfire so badly. So I returned to United and the Third Division until the approach of the transfer deadline suddenly prompted Everton to come back. I met Kendall along with my agent Gerry Webster at Birch services off the M62. Not exactly a top class hotel as you'd expect if he was really desperate to get me. Perhaps he thought he didn't need to serve up the expensive treatment for a Third Division player. He put his cards on the table like this. "What would you rather do: play for Everton in the First Division or Sheffield United in the Third?" He wasn't prepared for my answer: "Sheffield United in the Third!" There was some truth in what I was saying because I wasn't that bothered who I played for as long as I was in the team – but, yes, I was deliberately being stubborn and ignoring the obvious choice.

I wasn't that impressed with Kendall's offer of a £10,000

signing on fee and £500 a week. I told him my two-year deal at Bramall Lane came complete with a £25,000 signing on fee each season and I was also being paid the same amount to play two divisions lower. I wanted £50,000 to sign on plus £1,000 a week, but he wasn't for budging. I walked out of the meeting despite Gerry's brief attempts to get me to reconsider. Those were early days as far as agents were concerned and Gerry was more like a true insurance rep than the hawks who hike their clients to the highest bidders today. Until I suddenly said it was time to 'fuck off out of here' the guy had barely said a word. There was no way I was going to change my mind in any case. That was the end for me and agents; they weren't the force in the game they are now – Big Jack had just refused to deal with them – and, although I was still on good terms with Gerry, I never went down that line again after eventually leaving Sheffield.

I walked out of that modest café and into a flurry of national newspaper headlines having a go at 'greedy Curran'. The hacks may have been more generous had they known Everton were offering me a lesser deal than my current club – on the other hand would they have cared about the truth when they'd got a good story? I'm not anti-media like many players. I enjoyed writing my column for the *Sheffield Star*, chatting to local journalists and some of the better national ones. I still only have to lift up a phone to get my name into the newspapers and on the TV and Radio if I want to. But I'm also not naïve. There's a big difference between a 'good story' and the whole truth. The criticism hurt me more than a little. Yes, my shoulders were broad enough to cope and very few things in this strange life really worry me. But that isn't the point. It hurt because it misrepresented me to the fans and the football world in general. I wanted to sign for Everton; I just expected a better deal than I was already enjoying at a Third Division club.

Seeing out that season with Sheffield United was one of my hardest times in football. I didn't want to be there and knew

Ian Porterfield didn't want me there either. The team wasn't playing particularly well and for the first time in my career I wasn't enjoying my football. Thankfully, Everton came calling yet again at the beginning of the following campaign. The team was still falling below expectations and Kendall had no hesitation in meeting my asking prices. The deal meant that, with bonuses, I would clear £1,000 a week, the best deal in my playing career. It was good money and I appreciated it but nothing compared with the footballers of today. I was never going to be able to make a fortune and retire as a result but then an honest day's work does nobody any harm.

Joining Everton permanently promised to be a great new start for me. Having been such a favourite during my loan spell, I knew the fans were on my side. They were expecting me to give the team another boost and I was excited at being back in the big time permanently for the first time since Southampton. Reproducing the form I'd shown on loan over a consistent period could even have resurrected my hopes of playing for England. But, for the second time in my career, the injury jinx struck – and took the wind completely out of my sails.

I'd made my first appearance in a 3-0 midweek defeat at Ipswich before lining up against West Brom on September 10 1983. I don't remember much about the match itself – which finished in a disappointing scoreless draw – apart from what seemed like an innocuous incident that wrecked my season. The ball was played through to me and it looked as if I was going through one-on-one with the Albion goalkeeper. But as I gathered pace I pulled up sharply, rather like when pulling a hamstring. The pain was quite bad and there was no way I could continue, so I limped off to be replaced by Kevin Richardson. Nobody, including me, thought the injury was too serious but there then followed weeks of frustration as the medics tried to work out what was wrong. Eventually, they diagnosed it as a thigh strain but said that, because I also had a blood clot, I couldn't be operated on. Some Everton staff thought I was putting it on but, although I had no problem jogging, the sharp pain returned as soon as I tried to sprint. They obviously didn't know me very well. As far as I was concerned, this was a return of my Forest injury nightmare. I'd just got a chance to rebuild my career at a fantastic club, got myself into the team and in one moment I was out of action and watching the season pass me by. I'd have given anything to get back on the pitch quickly.

Fortunately, Everton physio John Clinkard believed in me and recommended to the club that I should go to Harley Street in London to see a specialist there. New technology meant they could take a better look at the injury and I was told it was a knife and fork job. So, after being sidelined for a lengthy spell waiting for this news, I then faced another comparable spell of recuperation after the operation. But at least I now knew I was on the mend.

It was April 7 1984 – nearly seven months after the West Brom incident – before I pulled on a first team shirt again at Luton Town. So I missed out on the time when the Everton machine really clicked into action, making it all the harder for me to get back into the starting line up.

Yet there were still very low moments along the way for the lads that season, leading up to the night the media have always insisted was the turning point for Howard Kendall at Everton – a League Cup quarter final tie at Oxford United's ramshackle Manor Ground on January 18. We had already lost 1-0 at home to Luton and 2-0 at Leicester, followed by another shattering blow for local morale – a 3-0 battering at Anfield. The media were convinced that, save for Inchy's late equaliser at Oxford to deny the home side a famous victory, Kendall would have been out on his ear and the subsequent glory days at Goodison may never have happened. But, like a few years later when a Mark Robins winner in an FA Cup tie at Forest allegedly saved Fergie's bacon, he went on to become one of the most successful managers of the modern era.

They may well have been right – in both cases. Certainly

it would have taken Howard more than a few drinks to get over the embarrassment of losing to Oxford – and that added to our inconsistent league form would probably have cost him the last of his lives even at a club where the fans were so desperate for him to succeed.

I'll tell you the day I think changed Everton's history and it came when I saw an emotional Peter Reid at training. I'd established a good friendship with Reidy and it just happened to be a day when I was asked to report in to check how I was doing with my recovery. I couldn't believe my ears when Reidy told me Everton had received an offer of £60,000 from Burnley and Kendall was all for accepting it. Reidy was also keen on the move. Don't get me wrong, this wasn't about friendship – this was football madness. I went straight in to see Kendall with more urgent things than my injury on my mind. "Why are you thinking about selling Reidy? He's the best midfield player at this football club," I said, taking the boss by surprise. How much value he put on my opinion I don't know. He certainly didn't ask for it, but got it nevertheless. All I do know is that keeping Reidy was one of the best decisions he ever made and played a very big part in the success we enjoyed whilst I was at Goodison Park. He was a terrific player, good enough to win 13 full caps for England and become the master of the Everton engine room. He was ultra competitive, a good passer of the ball and the guy who made the team tick. He was a very, very good player and – but for one missing link – could have even deserved the title of 'great'. Reidy lacked a yard of pace to get away from opponents and provide more of a goal threat. But then it's ok for a greyhound to talk!

The Oxford escape was game three in a 13-match unbeaten run that not only took the lads up the First Division but to the verge of Wembley in the League Cup and into the last eight of the FA Cup. Even when we finally lost – 1-0 at Aston Villa – it didn't matter too much as we'd already secured a two-goal lead from the first leg and the result took us to the League

Cup final and a tasty meeting with our noisy Merseyside neighbours. I fought a desperate fight to be in contention for Wembley as at last my injury began to subside. I managed to play two reserve games and one for the A team in a bid to force myself into Kendall's squad but it was always going to be too little too late. Kendall kept the door open for me for as long as possible but, after I'd failed to find my real form in a reserve defeat at Barnsley, he named his 14-man squad and I wasn't in it. So, frustratingly, I was a mere Wembley spectator as we drew 0-0 in front of a full house of 100,000 people before sitting down in front of my TV to see us lose 1-0 in the midweek replay at Maine Road.

It was a measure of how much Kendall still rated me, however, that he had one eye on getting me back for another big occasion – the FA Cup semi final against my old club Saints on April 14. It was a tight call but after a few more reserve outings – something I wasn't too accustomed to during my career – I made my return at Luton just a week before the cup tie. It was a successful afternoon, too, as we took revenge on David Pleat's team 3-0. I ran the gauntlet of the Kenilworth Road fans by having my say as Mal Donaghy, the Northern Ireland international, got sent off. I was hit on the inside of my leg by a missile thrown from the crowd for my trouble. My mate Inchy got himself a couple of goals before I put over the cross for Derek Mountfield to flick home a third.

Just 48 hours later we had another game at Goodison Park against Arsenal. It wasn't the most vital of our season as we were still only mid-table and our main focus was on trying to win some silverware but it meant everything to me. Getting through another 90 minutes in a 0-0 draw against a Gunners side, including England full back Kenny Sansom and with my former Forest colleague Tony Woodcock partnering Paul Mariner up front, was great. I was ready to do battle against the Saints.

The semi final was played at Highbury in front of more than 46,000 excited fans and gave me another chance to get one over on McMenemy who was still in charge of Southampton. Like many semi finals, it was a tight, nervy game with two of the very best goalkeepers, Nev and Shilts, able to keep their goals intact for almost the whole afternoon.

After the two comeback games in rapid succession and an exhausting and tense semi final, my legs were beginning to flag and I was aware that Kendall was preparing to haul me off to put on fresh legs with the prospect of extra time fast approaching. Then we won a free kick on the right hand side and I prepared to take what could well have been my last kick of the tie. Derek Mountfield got a flick on and there was Inchy squeezing home the winning goal with just three minutes left on the clock. The feeling was amazing. I remember sliding into my knees in celebration as if I'd scored myself. Everton were back at Wembley, I was back at Wembley and all the frustration and hard work suddenly seemed worthwhile again.

After the narrow miss against Liverpool, this gave us the perfect chance to get our hands on a trophy. We really fancied ourselves to win the cup providing we got past Saints as the other semi was between teams from the lower divisions – Elton John and Graham Taylor's Watford versus Plymouth Argyle. Hearing that Watford had come through didn't dampen our enthusiasm. Getting myself fit and back into the Everton team was exciting enough – now I could make up for defeat in my only previous Wembley appearance against Forest by getting my hands on the 'real' cup, the one everyone wanted to win.

It called for a serious celebration when we got back to Merseyside and a number of the lads went clubbing in Southport on a night that highlighted how the press could make life very difficult for footballers. I was there with Andy Gray, Bales and Inchy and the drink and the chat was flowing. Inchy was trying his level best to interest the girls in his winning goal while the rest of us were just trying to interest the girls. Andy came back from the bar with a couple of bottles of champagne and poured out drinks for our group. A pretty girl then pushed her way into our group in an attempt to get herself a free drink. Andy refused and out of the corner of my eye I saw her try to push her glass into his face. I put my hand up to protect my mate and the glass shattered cutting the girl's arm. The result was we all got interviewed by the police and the papers got another story about drunken footballers causing trouble on a night out. Yet all we were actually doing was enjoying a drink, a dance and hopefully some action after winning a very important match. We kept ourselves to ourselves, apart from the women we were chatting to, and the incident was caused by the young girl trying to barge her way in.

With just over a month to go until the big game itself against Watford, the boss wanted to get more games into my legs. It was a good plan, but may have cost me the chance to play in the biggest game of my life. The irony of the fixture computer sent us to The Dell the following Tuesday night for a First Division game in which David Armstrong got a couple of goals as we went down 3-1. Games continued to come thick and fast as I played 90 minutes the following Saturday in a 2-1 defeat at Sunderland and 48 hours later in a 2-0 home victory over Wolves.

All was going well as I lined up at Carrow Road against Norwich City on the Saturday, just three weeks before Wembley. That was where disaster struck as I pulled up with a pulled hamstring I knew instantly would keep me out of the FA Cup final. Bally's words came back loud and clear; I'd taken home my slice of Wembley turf after that League Cup defeat against Forest – and was destined never to return there. The League Cup was the League Cup – a big competition and one of the biggest days of my football life – but the FA Cup was everything in those days. Ever since watching at home when Everton broke my heart by coming back from the dead and defeating Wednesday, I'd dreamed of going out on the hallowed turf and playing in the most important date in the domestic football calendar. I'd come so close, yet so far. I'd won my injury battle, got back into the first team, played in the semi final and kept my place. I honestly think I was in line to play against Watford.

Did I play too many games too quickly? Yes, with the benefit of hindsight. Had I been used more sparingly after a long lay-off, I might be writing this looking at my FA Cup winner's medal. Do I blame Howard Kendall or any of his backroom staff? Not at all. They wanted me to play as much as I did. They would have had to haul me bodily off the pitch. Sadly, we didn't have the sports science and knowledge we have now. So instead of shaking hands with royalty and being watched by millions as I fulfilled one of my football dreams, I was in my usual Cup Final position – watching the game on TV. I preferred to do that rather than actually be there to be honest with the nearest I got to being part of the action coming next evening when Inchy came round to see me in Southport to show off his medal. We went for a drink in a nearby bar and my mate was still visibly shaking with emotion as he described what it was like to be part of a winning FA Cup final team.

Naturally I'd been thrilled when Sharpy put us in front and Andy Gray manhandled his way past Watford goalkeeper Steve Sherwood to head the clincher in the second half. It was great to be with a club that won the FA Cup; I just wish I'd been a part of it. Nevertheless, I was pleased for Gray, one of the most important signings Kendall ever made. What a guy! Blimey, his knees were more knackered than mine – and that was saying something. But he was as brave as an ox, as he showed scoring that controversial goal and on countless other important occasions. No matter what state his body was in, he always put it on the line on the pitch. Had he remained fitter, he could have been one of the great strikers. As it was, he was an extremely good one and a key part in Everton's success story. It was much the same off the pitch too. He always put his heart on the line with the women. I've never known someone fall in love as often as he did – that's not a criticism, just the way he was. He'd get involved with his women whereas I 'loved and left'. We are all different, after all.

Socially, I was having a great time at Everton. Again women weren't hard to find. I met this beautiful woman and being out with Inchy one night got talking about whether we should have a double act, if you see what I mean. "You're joking," he said. "Don't you know who she is?" He whispered it to me and I'm not going to even whisper her name to you to save her reputation – but let's say she was a young woman with connections to the club. I went on to have a sexual relationship with her for about six weeks and came close to a very difficult situation when it broke down. She started phoning the flat in Southport which I was sharing with Lorraine causing me to fall back on a classic footballer's excuse. I told Lorraine that the woman was probably a fan who liked the look of me from watching the games. "But how did she get your number?" Lorraine asked. I said that such people are always capable of getting information if they told a few white lies. Luckily, I got away with another whopper!

Bales became a great mate and, to be fair, one of the best drinkers in the side. Those were days when the lads used to spend time in the players' lounge having a few jars after the game – and the keener drinkers took it from there. Bales was on the booze most weekends, leaving us with a challenge to try to hide the evidence when we reported back to training on the Monday morning. I usually picked him up and, even with a lacing of garlic to try to mask the smell, sometimes there was no way he was going to get away with it. So Reidy, Inchy and I took Bales to see John Clinkard and he'd usually go along with the story Bales had picked up a slight strain and it wouldn't be wise for him to take part in training. Sometimes there was no way he was up to it.

Bales was also responsible for introducing me to a new experience of a sexual kind on a tour of Switzerland. We were sitting down and relaxing when the full back suddenly asked me out of the blue for £50. When I asked why, he started talking about this fantastic blonde woman in the town. I replied that I wasn't into prostitution, so he took a different approach – saying I should come along as well and, if I didn't agree she was worth every penny, he'd pay me back. I must admit I was a bit nervous walking down the street – and Bales got the shakes too when I grabbed him by the arm to stop him in his tracks. I'd just seen a taxi pull up and out got a member of the Everton hierarchy who was then walking up the stairs to her flat sporting a couple of bottles of champagne! Sheepishly, we disappeared into a nearby café and waited our turn. An hour or so later we saw the man come out with a wide grin on his face and we went in to see her. All I'm saying is that Bales proved to be a very good judge and a very good businessman!

Another thing that made me laugh was when Kendall finally decided to bin Bales the drinker, he brought in Pat Van Den Hauwe as his replacement. If it was obvious to everyone Bales loved his pints but Van Den Hauwe was a secret tippler of the highest quality. Like Bales, he was also a damned good, fierce tackling left back.

Mind you, Monday morning was usually a pretty delicate time for the boss as well as some of the players. Even in those days, Howard loved a drink – and then a whole lot more. Wine, shorts and most other things alcoholic hit the spot for him and he'd often go for a sauna on a Monday morning to try to sweat it out of his system. Not that I'm having a go at Kendall – not at all. The bloke was pure quality and proved to be right up there among the celebrated bosses that I played for. They may not have looked alike or talked in the same way but there were similarities between Kendall and Cloughie, not least the fact both were genuine winners. Let's face it, between them there wasn't a competition they didn't win – from League Cups to European silverware, they scooped the lot.

One thing that always impresses the lads is when the gaffer looks the part on the training ground. Big Jack, as I've said, was the exact opposite but Howard Kendall won our respect when he took part in practice games and training. He and Colin Harvey were great. They were no longer in their prime but I could definitely get a sense just how good they were when they wore the royal blue shirt. Harvey, to be fair, didn't get his kit on too often as he was suffering a lot of jip from his hips but Howard worked harder in training and practice games than most of the lads and his touch and passing were fantastic.

As a youngster he'd written himself into the record books by becoming the youngest ever player to appear in an FA Cup final when he lined up for his first club Preston North End in 1964 against West Ham United. The 1966 World Cup came too soon for him as we had that brilliant midfield of Bally, Bobby Charlton and Martin Peters but how he never won a senior cap is totally beyond me. I put him up there with Cloughie for a number of reasons. He was a great motivator and a great coach. People think it's all about coming into the dressing room, throwing tea cups and ranting and raving, but that isn't the case with the very best. Howard, like Cloughie, filled the lads with confidence. Then at half time he'd make some sensible observations about what was happening on the pitch. There'd be no tantrums or anything like that just good tips about how to improve our game in the second half.

We began the 1984-85 season in great spirits. After all, we'd just taken our first major step in ending Liverpool's domination by landing a trophy. The question now was could we turn our great cup form into a challenge for the First Division title? Our adventure in the European Cup Winners' Cup was also something new at a fairly late stage in my career. I was fit enough but the problem was how to get into a team purring like a Rolls Royce, particularly as I was in direct competition on the right flank with Trevor Steven. He'd been a relative youngster at 20 when Kendall snapped him up from Burnley and initially struggled to fulfill his obvious promise but, once in his stride, he was a class act. A totally different wide player to me, Steven had the talent to play more than 200 matches for Everton as well as winning 36 caps for England.

I made a fair few appearances early on in a campaign that was to become one of the most famous in this great club's history. It was difficult to believe that, after Brucie Grobbelaar had given us the bonus of a Charity Shield success over our closest rivals with an own goal at Wembley, we began a league season in which we eventually swept aside everyone with a 4-1 defeat at Goodison Park against Spurs. That, at least, gave me the chance to start in the second match at The Hawthorns where, despite another spot kick from Inchy, we again went down 2-1. I came on as a substitute for Kevin Richardson in the next two Goodison clashes, a 1-1 draw against Ipswich, followed by a welcome first home win over Coventry when Steven and Sharpy got us out of trouble with goals in the last 20 minutes after Terry Gibson had put the Sky Blues ahead.

My first ever taste of European football was a strange one – and again there was little indication of the team's glory to come as we struggled to a 0-0 draw against University College, Dublin, in front of an Irish crowd of just 9,750. I came on for Steven for the last 20 minutes as we strove in vain to make a breakthrough. I then played the full 90 minutes of a surprisingly tense return game a fortnight later when just over 16,000 Goodison fans nearly saw us stumble out of Europe. Sharpy edged us ahead after 10 minutes but, as the floodgates refused to open, we were left on a knife edge as an equaliser would have seen us go out on away goals. In the end we were relieved to avoid an embarrassing exit as we squeezed through to the second round 1-0 on aggregate. Reidy recently said on TV the Irish minnows gave Everton their toughest test in Europe that season – and he wasn't joking.

There was no shortage of goals when I made a short and disastrous appearance as a last gasp sub at Watford. There were nine in all at Vicarage Road with Everton eventually winning 5-4. Inchy got himself a double as did Derek Mountfield – shame one of them was in his own net. Among the scorers for

Graham Taylor's men was John Barnes, who was to become one of the best players of his generation at Liverpool. He was on the left flank supplying ammunition for the likes of Luther Blissett, who also won England recognition. I came on in the 90th minute but still had time to get myself sent off! I just couldn't help myself when, after being on the pitch for a full 60 seconds, I turned round and gave a poor linesman a volley of verbal abuse over a throw-in decision. It was completely stupid and it put paid to my first team chances for a while. That was a pity as I would have loved to have played against the Blades and put one over Ian Porterfield in the League Cup. A 4-0 thrashing at Goodison eased us through 6-2 on aggregate – another massacre!

By the time we went to Anfield for our first league meeting of the season with the old enemy I was out of the team – not that I allowed that to ruin my enjoyment! I remember talking to Kendall in training as he reminded the lads about Liverpool's main threats. "What are you worried about, boss? We've got some fantastic players here," I told him. One of our greatest assets without doubt was Neville Southall. This was an era when England had terrific goalkeepers in Ray Clemence and Shilts competing for our number one spot but, in my view, Wales had the best goalie in Europe, if not the world, in Nev. It's difficult to put into words but he was one bloke who genuinely had an aura about him. Some goalies can be intimidated by strikers; with him, it was very much the other way around. He dominated his penalty area with his personality and physicality. He loved to come off his line, punch the ball away with one hand and the lights out of the opposition's centre forward with the other. He gave the impression he never expected to concede a goal and that definitely affected our opponents. They must have felt they needed to strike the ball absolutely perfectly to get past his imposing frame and, more often than not, missed the target altogether. I'll tell you another thing about Neville – he could certainly play a bit too. He was one of those goalkeepers who enjoyed coming out of goal in five-a-sides and showing he had more than his fair share of skill on the ball as well as gloves of iron. It gives the defence – and the whole team – incredible confidence to have someone of his quality and presence behind them. It was tough enough to get past a back four in which Gary Stevens, Derek Mountfield and Kevin Ratcliffe played 117 league games between them. But most impressive of all was Neville Southall who never missed a second of our 63 games in all competitions. Until I saw Peter Schemeichel play for Manchester United, I don't think I'd ever seen a better number one.

I was living in a flat in Southport in a prime location above the Café Gardens. There was a Chinese on the corner too so it was just perfect! In the week before the Anfield game I was taking a stroll along the front with Bales when my eyes spied a vision of beauty coming in the other direction. Blonde, vivacious, busty – you get the picture! We both continued walking in opposite directions for a few yards before I turned round and saw her staring back. "Hello, handsome!" she said. That was for me not you, Bales! We both sat down for a coffee with her and I started to give her some chat. Much to my delight, she agreed to meet up on the Saturday as I knew I wouldn't be playing. I then gave Inchy a bit of banter. "When you kick off against Liverpool, think of me, mate – I will be shagging a blue-eyed blonde!"

We met as planned and everything else went as planned too. The sex was electric, more than making up for my disappointment at missing the big match. She knew I was an Everton footballer but was a little surprised when, in the middle of our love-making, I turned on the radio just in time for kick off. "What are you doing that for?" she asked. Well, it was a good question! I told her I was interested in the game and kept the radio on throughout the afternoon. I don't think the blonde was too impressed but the words of the radio commentator made my day complete. "There's Adrian Heath kicking off with a huge smile on his face," he said. As I confirmed with Inchy afterwards, he was thinking of me and how I'd be enjoying myself rather than plotting a way past Mark Lawrenson and Alan Hanson and co. That was the afternoon on which Sharpy scored an absolutely fantastic goal from fully 35 yards into the top corner to give us a 1-0 victory. Mind you, my scoring wasn't too bad either!

We were really beginning to take off now as we thrashed Manchester United 5-0 at Goodison Park with Sheedy getting a couple before completing a quick 'double' by knocking them out of the League Cup 2-1 at Old Trafford. Inter Bratislava were brushed aside 4-0 on aggregate in Europe in the middle of a run of four successive wins without Nev having to bend his back and pick the ball out of our net. Then a mini-slump, starting with a surprise League Cup exit at Grimsby and three winless league games, including a 4-2 thumping at Norwich, gave me a sniff of a return when Cloughie came into town again with Forest. I only saw 10 minutes of action as Andy Gray rested his battered knees after we had trounced mid-table Forest into oblivion. Sharpy (2), Sheedy and Steven had already settled the points before I came on and Reidy made it a high five in the last minute.

We were top of the league and on top of the world and, although Chelsea briefly burst our bubble by edging a 4-3 thriller three days before Christmas, there was no stopping us after that as we went on a 28-game unbeaten run in all competitions including 24 victories and only 13 scowls from Nev when the ball went past him. Christmas was celebrated in style with four wins in nine days and I was delighted to get two full games and play my part in a couple of important victories. I came in for the injured Andy Gray at Portman Road which gave me the chance to play in my favourite position, up front, in the First Division for the first time in my career. It was my challenge that gave Sharpy the opportunity to net his second goal to clinch the points. Luton then came to Goodison with us needing to win by five clear goals on New Year's Day to regain top spot. I could have done it all on my own as I had three chances in the early stages but the best I managed was hitting the woodwork. Trevor Steven got both our goals in a 2-1 victory and again I felt I'd done reasonably well.

It wasn't enough to get me a regular place as coming off the bench – and staying on the field this time – in a 4-0 victory at home to Watford was my only first team action for a while as we eventually reeled off nine victories on the trot. Massive interest in the FA Cup was shown by the fact that more than 37,000 saw us beat Donny and there were 10,000 more on the Goodison gate for the fifth round tie against giantkilling non leaguers Telford who fought gamely before going down 3-0. Kendall still had me in mind for Europe, however, and I got the call to start as Andy Gray destroyed Dutch visitors Fortuna Sittard with a hat trick in the first leg of the quarter final at Goodison. I then played in a fairly relaxed second leg a fortnight later as Reidy and Sharpy completed a 5-0 aggregate victory.

That brought German giants Bayern Munich out of the hat for the semi finals – and an episode that not only ended my Goodison career but has to go down as one of my worst ever decisions. We were training on Merseyside before flying to Germany for the first leg. I knew both Kevin Sheedy and Andy Gray were likely to miss out through injuries and that gave me a better chance of being in Kendall's starting line up. Sometimes you get an idea, however, from the way the session is organised whether you are going to be in the team – and I didn't like what I was seeing. So, after the session ended, I went up to the manager and asked him straight whether I was in the side. He said he hadn't yet made up his mind and would be announcing the side nearer to kick off but I didn't believe him. I told him I wasn't going to go to the airport and, despite Inchy, Reidy and Bales warning me how stupid I was being, I stuck to my guns. Bales was particularly worried as I had his kit in my car so didn't want me to drive off with it! Anyway I sorted Bales out, then rang a woman I'd been going out with for a couple of weeks. We met up for lunch and I forgot all about the Cup Winners' Cup, Munich and all things football as I stayed at her fantastic house – she and her husband had bought it off one of the Liverpool lads – for a couple of days. Her husband, by the way, was working in Saudi Arabia. She ran me a bath of pink champagne and we made bubbles in the most natural of ways!

To be honest, nobody could have doubted Kendall's tactics. He put Trevor Steven behind lone striker Sharpy and had Alan Harper and Kevin Richardson playing with defensive discipline along the flanks as we ground out a 0-0 draw in Munich, which was regarded as virtually a perfect away result back then. We now had a great chance in the return leg at Goodison Park but I was preparing to face the flak when Kendall and co got back home. He didn't say a great deal about it to my face but the Liverpool Echo got to know I'd refused to travel so I was in deep water. As I've been writing this, the Carlos Tevez episode has been attracting a great deal of attention after he allegedly refused to come off the bench for Roberto Mancini's Manchester City in a Champions League tie. That prompted Kendall to recall in a radio interview that two Everton players did a similar thing in his day but, to his credit, he didn't name names.

Unlike Tevez who was allowed to return to the fold even after disappearing to Argentina, there was never going to be any way back for me at Goodison Park after that – and quite rightly. The manager, who wasn't one to hold grudges, was largely fine with me and I continued to train with the first team but I was never selected again either in the side or on the bench. A crazy decision had once again sealed my exit from a great football club and I was the obvious loser. If I could turn back the clock I'd be in Munich in a flash, but the damage was done. In my defence, it just tells you how much I cared about playing – about being in the first team. Like at Forest when I battered Cloughie's office door down, I hated being out of the Everton side even though it was virtually impossible for Kendall to change it.

The lads went on to reach another FA Cup final without me as they beat Luton Town 2-1 after extra time in a tense semi final at Villa Park three days after returning from Munich. Kevin Sheedy and Derek Mountfield got the goals that booked a dream final against Manchester United. I then watched wondering yet again what might well have been as we lifted the Cup Winners' Cup on a fantastic night for Everton Football Club in Rotterdam. Andy Gray got the party under way before Steven and Sheedy ensured it was goodnight Rapid Vienna as we clinched a 3-1 victory. The cup double wasn't to be however. We went into the final as hot favourites against United, all the more so after their defender Kevin Moran made unfortunate history by becoming the first player ever to get sent off in an FA Cup final for a challenge on Reidy. Norman Whiteside ruined our day by curling a 20-yarder past Southall to win the trophy for United.

I knew my opportunities would be limited if I stayed at Goodison Park and met Kendall to ask for a free transfer. I'd just applied for the job as player manager of Fourth Division Halifax Town and they'd offered it to me. But the manager insisted he wanted a fee. I went back again at the end of the season and this time played my joker. I came up with a killer line to persuade him to change his mind – one that, unlike everything else in this book of confessions – I'm choosing to keep to myself out of respect for a truly brilliant manager.

By this time, the job at The Shay had come and gone – something I regret to this day. Perhaps if Kendall had let me go first time, I could have become a Football League manager and built another successful career in the game off-the-field. There's no point in thinking about it any further because we'll never ever know. I've never had a second chance to manage at that level – although where there's life and a hell of a lot of passion and knowledge, there's still hope! Instead Third Division Huddersfield Town had offered me the chance to continue my playing career at Leeds Road. So the next leg of my varied and unpredictable football journey took me back once again to Yorkshire.

As for Kendall, I still have the highest regard for him. So what was the secret of his great success as a manager? Like Cloughie, it isn't that easy to put into words a feeling that you know to be true. Kendall was a great manager. To turn around Everton as he did after coming under pressure that would have broken a lesser man was a fantastic achievement. In those two full seasons I spent with him at Goodison Park, he won the First Division title, the FA Cup and the European Cup Winners' Cup as well as getting to two other finals. Howard, again like Cloughie, didn't spend endless time building up the opposition and making us feel inferior. He wanted us to be relaxed and confident in our own ability when Saturday came. The training was first class. We practiced our ball skills rather than running marathons and there was plenty of attention to detail to ensure we were well prepared.

If only history could be re-written, I've no doubt Kendall could have dominated Europe for several years with that side. We were virtually unbeatable as a unit and were only just coming into our prime with that European triumph. Obviously what happened at Hysel in 1985 when 39 Juventus fans lost their lives before the European Cup final against Liverpool was a human tragedy – and everything else means very little compared with that. But it was sad and frustrating from a sporting point of view that it prevented Everton from going on and quite possibly winning the big one – the European Cup.

Kendall's frustration with the ban on English clubs from European competitions also played a part in his eventual departure from Goodison in 1987 when he left to manage Athletic Bilbao in Spain. Thanks to him, I have a First Division winners' medal I will cherish for the rest of my life. I just wish I'd been fit and sensible enough to have played a greater part.

8

A Real Matter of Life and Death

"Football's not a matter of life and death – it's more important than that."

Bill Shankley, Liverpool's legendary manager.

FOOTBALL fans love that, don't we? It sums up how we feel about our clubs. Win a game and we're on top of the world – me included – lose and everything seems dark and bleak. Until the next game, at least . . . The only problem I have with Shanks' well-known quote is that it just isn't true! If you're lucky or young enough never to have been seriously ill or dealt with the death of a loved one, you may still believe it. But, once you have, it'll probably change your outlook completely.

This sad tale starts with my last 'real' season as a footballer at Huddersfield Town in 1985-86. After working for a man as full of modern ideas as Kendall, it was back to Sergeant Major time as I played for Terriers boss Mick Buxton at Leeds Road. Spoiled by the great passing football at Goodison Park, I was back on familiar territory with Buxton preaching the long ball and trying to win it back once we'd hoofed it aimlessly from one end of the pitch to the other. But, despite the training being from the dark ages and Buxton's old fashioned man management style, I thoroughly enjoyed my season in the Second Division with Huddersfield, my 10th Football League club and a great one to play for.

I was struggling so badly with my knees I was never going to play a full season and I suffered a setback during what was one of the best days I had at Leeds Road. Any game against McMenemy was well worth winning to my mind and I made a great start to our match against Sunderland – who he was then managing – by scoring two first half goals. But then I limped off with a hamstring injury as we safely saw out a 2-0 victory and was sidelined for several weeks. Buxton brought me back for a Yorkshire derby, the Boxing Day clash with Barnsley, but it proved too soon as I was injured again and needed further time out. Only the bitter winter that put football in cold storage for several weeks limited the number of games I missed.

Personal highlights included putting one over a couple more clubs not on my Christmas card list. Leeds United had often been rivals during my travels and I lapped up scoring in a 3-1 victory in the derby against Eddie Gray's side. Curran, the showman, wasn't finished yet as I celebrated with a bow in front of the United supporters. I then repeated the gesture to all the other three sides of Leeds Road in a repeat of my reaction to the FA's crusade against hugging and kissing. Naughty, naughty, but well worth it!

Going back to Bramall Lane for the first and only time after my strange Sheffield United experience was always going to be a big day. The Blades had Peter Withe, my former Forest mate, leading their attack and for the first 45 minutes neither of us covered ourselves in glory. But, after the Blades had gone ahead with an own goal, I rolled back the years – and the jeers – by really having a crack at them in the second half. I didn't get myself on the scoresheet but played my part in our equaliser with a jinking run before laying on the cross for David Cox to clinch us a well-earned point and win a few more headlines from journalists who appreciated my history. Nothing against Hull City but I had some fun in that local derby too. Coming back from the cold I again proved my head wasn't just for chatting up birds. Dave Cowling put over a great first time cross and I grabbed the winner. Pity Big Jack wasn't there to see it!

There were some good lads in the Terriers' side. We had Brian Cox, the former Wednesday goalie; big Paul Jones, a true character and a former Bolton Wanderers hero, at centre back; Dale Tempest, the former Fulham striker; David Cowling on the opposite flank to me and Duncan Shearer, who'd joined us from Chelsea, up front. Buxton, to be fair, was a hard working manager typical of the bosses of his day. He'd bark out his orders and then sulk if things didn't go our way. At those times he wouldn't talk with anyone.

I clashed verbal swords with him when he gave a team talk before our match at Carlisle United. The guy went on and on for about 45 minutes, listing all the good things about each likely opponent. The left back could do this and we'd have to watch out for the centre half, the right winger . . . the whole damned lot, it seemed! Mick always ended his talk by asking whether we had any questions and that gave me my chance. "Just one thing, boss," I said. "Who are we playing today?" When he angrily answered, I went on: "I thought we were playing Brazil – this lot are so bloody good!" The lads laughed, enjoying the fact I had the guts to stand up to him. Not surprisingly, he wasn't happy and that probably helped him mark my card come the end of the season. I was known to the very last as the player who spoke out. So when Shearer was on the receiving end of Mick at his ranting and raving best despite us playing quite well at Blackburn, he asked whether I'd talk to the manager for him. That time, at least, I decided not to fight someone else's battle.

The end of the season brought the curtain down on my Huddersfield career and I was open to offers when I got a surprise phone call from a Greek club called Panionios. I must admit the only Greek teams I knew were AEK Athens and Olympiakos, but I found out they were another Athens-based club in the Greek First Division and wanted both me and Gary Owen, the former Manchester City midfielder, to bolster their team for the new season. Wages were about £600 a week and it seemed like a good adventure given I was nearing the end of my career. I'd always wanted to play abroad and, having enjoyed my brief fling in Sweden whilst at Wednesday, set out with my girlfriend Lorraine quite excited but not knowing what to expect. I joined them during pre-season and we toured Belgium playing friendlies and getting ourselves fit for the new campaign.

Lorraine and I were put up in a beautiful hotel in the middle of Athens and the weather was red hot but that was the very best part of this Greek package. I didn't know anyone else apart from Lorraine and Gary and not speaking a word of the language didn't make life any easier with the football.

Real doubts began to emerge after the first two or three weeks. At every other club I'd played for, wages were agreed then I got on with playing knowing the money would be paid. But I became aware my weekly wages weren't going through and the promises of officials that it would all be sorted out the following week started to wear thin. The league season in Greece was delayed a couple of weeks due to a players' strike – and I was soon planning one of my own. Gary asked my opinion whether we were going to get paid and I said I didn't think so. No explanation was given to any of us about the finances of the club so we didn't have a clue what was actually going on. I told Gary I'd give it one more week and, if we still hadn't received any money, I'd quit. I didn't go to Greece for the money but we were being taken for a ride here. Finally, after a couple of months, I set a deadline to check my bank and booked the next flight back home to England.

My version of a mini Greek tragedy was then followed by a kind offer from manager Brian Horton to come to Hull City where I played four games. Then, completely out of the blue, I got some very good and some very bad news. Finding out a massive club such as Sunderland wanted to sign me was fantastic – shame Lawrie McMenemy was in charge! I wouldn't have even bothered speaking with the club but Dad talked sense into me, insisting I should bite my tongue because I was very unlikely to get a better chance to carry on playing.

To be fair, McMenemy was happy to let bygones be bygones although he must have seen the interviews I'd given to the nationals about his management when I said he couldn't run a fish and chip shop. He always praised me as a player saying I was good enough to play for England if I could get my head right and, after all, he made a last minute attempt to keep me at Saints. It was he who had most to lose now from taking on a 30-year-old with a bad injury record. I was a typical panic signing managers often make when wanting to get bodies in to please the fans. So I signed a one-year deal at Roker Park.

The Weirsiders expected big things from McMenemy after what he'd achieved at Saints with a relatively unfashionable club. Winning an FA Cup, getting to a League Cup final and even taking the club to runners up in the First Division in 1984 made him one of the most talked about and sought after managers in English football. I knew, however, just how limited the guy really was. He tried the same formula that worked at The Dell – surround himself with experienced players who probably knew a great deal more about the game than he did; Eric Gates and George Burley, from Ipswich; Frankie Gray, formerly of Leeds and Forest; Palace striker Dave Swindlehurst and Gary Bennett, who played at Roker Park for 11 years, were all in that team. The fans were banking on players and a manager with such good reputations to restore them to the top flight.

Results weren't good at the start of the season and the fans were getting restless. I was playing regularly in a team that wasn't living up to our potential when, just a few weeks after I arrived at Roker Park, I took a surprise phone call from my sister-in-law Patsy. "Its bad news, I'm afraid," she said. "It's your Dad: he's got cancer." When you hear those words, your thoughts change instantly. Like everyone else I'd been looking forward to going to Birmingham City on the Saturday to try to get the win we needed to lift our season. But now a trip to St Andrews was the very last thing on my mind.

The news was very bad. Dad had been diagnosed with

cancer of the throat and given just a month to live. I wanted to spend as much of the short time he had left with him. Nothing else really mattered as we'd always been close and I loved Dad so much. From giving up his sleep to take me to Donny for the trial that gave me my first chance in the professional game to that very last piece of advice when he didn't want my stubbornness to rob me of a contract at Sunderland, he was always there for me in my career. But, more importantly, despite the break-up with Mum, he was there for me as a father and in our family life. Losing a loved one is one of the most painful things – if not the most painful – in the whole world. How can anyone lose sleep over whether their football team has won or lost over the weekend when they know what life and death is really about?

I went into the ground on the Friday morning and told McMenemy what was happening. I said my Dad had cancer, was dying and I needed to be with him. I didn't want to be considered for the Birmingham match and I would be away from the club. "For how long?" he asked. "Until afterwards" I replied, feeling very emotional. The manager wasn't happy but knew there was nothing he could do. I'd told him I was going and that was that. I'm not going to criticise him for his reaction but what happened next was something I can never forgive.

A few hard weeks went by for McMenemy and the boys as results continued to go against them, including a 2-0 defeat by Sheffield United. But, for me, that time was much, much harder. I spent as much of it as I possibly could by Dad's bedside. It was heartbreaking to see a man I recognised as strong look so pale, thin and yellow. We were losing him day by day, hour by hour and there was absolutely nothing any of us could do about it. It's difficult to describe what it feels like when someone you have been so close to can hardly remember your name or recognise you. Cancer is a cruel, cruel disease and I support anyone who can find a way to reduce the suffering it brings. David and Patsy were constantly there and all the brothers came when they could. It was both an awful and also very precious time, if you know what I mean. Given the same circumstances, I wouldn't hesitate to do exactly the same thing again – and that's from someone who genuinely loves his football.

Inevitably, I got a phone call from the football club. It was from Lou Chatterley, McMenemy's assistant, and I told him I wasn't coming back. Dad was living a little longer than the doctors had expected and my place was by his side. I'd done no training at all for several weeks and was in no fit state either physically or mentally to play a football match. Lou said I needed to get back into the swing of things as soon as possible as the team was still struggling and he wanted me to play in a home reserve match against Manchester City on the Tuesday night. I talked with David, who agreed I should show my face. Both he and his best friend Jack Hicks came along to support me. When I got to the ground, the lads brought me up-to-date with all the gossip – and it wasn't good. The fans were beginning to take their frustration out on McMenemy directly for all the club's troubles. Apparently they'd been pelting his prized gold Mercedes with stones, kicking it and tying to tip it over. Again, I'd ask how a few bad football results gives anyone the right to attack the manager's property? In the name of 'passion' all sorts of crazy things happen in this game.

It also wasn't rare for players to be booed when having a rough time. One of the younger Sunderland lads was coming in for a lot of abuse and Lou had dropped him down to the reserve side as he was unlikely to be featuring the following Saturday. But that was no insurance against the boo boys – not when around 3,500 to 4,000 fans came to watch the second team in action. The game got under way and I noticed the same lad was being barracked every time he touched the ball. Constant criticism was doing him no good at all as he was fast losing his confidence. Eventually we got a free kick and, although he would usually have taken it, he called me across and asked whether I'd do it instead. He was the guy under pressure but I lost it. I was so disgusted with the way the fans were treating him, I stuck two fingers up in the direction of the crowd. Next moment I was hauled off and could have no complaints. I'd not been in the right state of mind to play and that affected the way I reacted. But worse, far worse was to follow the embarrassment of being substituted. Two police officers arrested me in the tunnel for inciting the crowd.

I drove home that night angry about what had happened. It was nothing compared with what was happening back home, but it certainly didn't help. A couple of days later I picked up *The Sun* newspaper to read 'Sunderland sack Curran'. I'd not had a meeting or even a phone call from the manager. I read about his decision in the national press at an incredibly emotional time in my personal life before receiving a letter a few days later confirming the news that to all intents and purposes my playing career was over.

No Sunderland fan knows to this day what really happened. Until now. It was probably the least of their worries as I'd only played a handful of games and would be quickly forgotten. But I will never forgive McMenemy for the way he treated me. He used a moment of madness when I was very vulnerable to show he was the boss. Curran, the bad boy, stuck two fingers up to the fans and the big man showed everyone he wasn't taking any nonsense. Obviously he thought he'd score a few points with people who were increasingly getting on his back.

There was no mention in any of the newspapers about the hell I was going through. I still don't know how Sunderland explained my absence during those few weeks – and I don't really care. I've got nothing at all against the football club – playing for Sunderland was a great privilege and, although I wasn't there for long, I was left with a lasting impression of just how big a club it is. It wasn't Sunderland who let me down but Lawrie McMenemy, the same genial chap who used to charm everyone in his many TV interviews but was barely recognisable in real life. It was a bitter irony, too, when

I think about it that one reserve match involving Sunderland played such a big part in launching my professional career – and another one effectively ended it. Maybe someone up there was blowing the final whistle on me.

I didn't have the emotional reserves to take in the full consequences of McMenemy's action back then as I had the far more important matter of Dad's condition on my mind. The following week was terrible. I barely slept at all as I sat by his bedside, waiting for the inevitable. Then one night my oldest brother John said he would take over for a few hours as I needed to get some rest. Early next morning he woke me up with the news – Dad had just passed peacefully away.

I was gutted I wasn't there with him when he died. It was, however, just one of those sad things. I'm glad I spent time with him when I could and did what the majority of people would do in the same circumstances. It wouldn't have mattered a jot whether I'd still been a Wednesday player or even been on Manchester United's books – football is football, but your loved ones are what really matter. Shanks was a great football manager, who started the revival of one of the world's most successful clubs. But he was way off the mark when he said what he did. There would always be another Saturday – even for a 31-year-old with battered knees – but I will never have another Dad. God bless him.

If I did anything I regret in the whole sad episode it was going to that damned reserve match. I should have realised no good could come from it. I'm sure I wasn't alone in being treated so insensitively in my time of need. Clubs used to keep a lid on things and personal matters rarely made the headlines like they do today when you hear about players being given time off to attend the birth of babies and having the choice whether to play when they have a personal crisis. As in many issues we live and learn.

Sunderland wasn't, as it turned out, quite the end of my professional career which actually spluttered to a halt the following season. Grimsby Town boss Bobby Roberts called to ask me to help him out as he was struggling for players in his Third Division side. I ended up making 13 appearances, including a couple as substitute, and in all honesty the sea air and fish and chips were probably better for me than continuing to wreck my battered knees. My most memorable moment at Grimsby wasn't on the pitch at all but when I went to see a specialist with talk of another cortisone injection in the air. He told me straight that, if I continued to play any competitive sports, let alone football, I'd end up a cripple. He was right too – but it was already too late to save me from a painful future. I just had time to end my Football League career playing one and only one game as a substitute for Chesterfield on Saturday, March 12 1988, ironically in a 1-1 draw at Grimsby Town. Again, I was more or less doing a favour for manager Kevin Randall – and it backfired to a certain extent.

Folklore has it that I was booed onto the pitch by both sets of supporters – as I hadn't done much for Grimsby and Spireites fans still remembered our feisty encounters in Wednesday's promotion season. I don't remember my reception being that bad, to be honest, but it was a little sad that my professional career ended in a limp manner. The fans of both clubs probably thought I was a big time Charlie ending his career in a lower league without a care in the world, but they couldn't have been more wrong. If you've understood anything I've written, you'll realise I was an honest lad who just wanted to play, even when my body was telling me I shouldn't have been anywhere near a football field.

Chesterfield were my 13th and final league club – a record bettered at the time only by Les Roberts, a much-travelled player in the 1920s, who appeared for 16 clubs in as many seasons. For the sake of Les, I hope the fans in his day didn't taunt him as a 'gypo' because, although I'm the first to admit I moved too often and two quickly early in my career, the taunt hurt. To be fair, my number of clubs was exaggerated by that muddled ending in which I spread my last 26 appearances among Hull City, Sunderland, Grimsby and Chesterfield when my body was defying gravity. According to the statisticians, I played some 424 games and scored 77 goals – or one in every 5.5 matches which isn't bad, particularly considering I played the vast majority on the right flank. Had I persuaded managers more often to pick me in my preferred position as a striker, or been able to retain the penalty taking responsibilities I had briefly at Forest and Wednesday, I'd have topped the century mark with plenty to spare.

Looking back now, I'm pleased that I played most games – 138 – and scored most goals – 39 – for Sheffield Wednesday, the club I've supported as man and boy. I only wish I'd stayed long enough to have pulled on an Owls shirt in the top flight but can blame only myself for making such a daft move to Sheffield United. I will always look back fondly to Donny Rovers, the club that gave the boy from Kinsley his big chance, and to Forest, where I first came to national prominence and had the honour of playing for one of the greatest of all managers in Cloughie. My short time on the south coast remains memorable for providing me with my one and only chance to play at Wembley and become a team mate and close buddy of the brilliant Alan Ball. Then there was Everton, by far the best team and club I ever played for and with whom I got a First Division winner's medal, even though my spell there was ravaged by injury. It all added up to a case of falling short as far as my ambition of playing for England was concerned and I know many will say that about my career as a whole. I'm the first to acknowledge I could have been more successful had I made better decisions at crucial times but, hopefully, being a maverick had its compensations in that I left some good memories and entertained supporters – which is often underestimated.

I did manage to fulfill my last ambition in football before hanging up my boots completely – playing in the same team again as my brother David. He was still playing for Kinsley Boys all those years later after having rejected the chance to go into professional football with both Forest and Wednesday. We were still as close as we've always been but hadn't played in the same team for 16 years – something I wanted to put right when I had the chance.

Adding together his goals in Saturday and Sunday football, he was definitely into four figures. Remember all the excitement when Pele, the legendary Brazilian, scored his 1,000th goal – well my brother topped that by a long way. When you think about it, we were quite alike even though I always wanted to play professional and he didn't. The similarity was purely and simply our love for playing the game. David turned down Cloughie and Wednesday because he was happy playing football with his mates and working as a miner. Why not? Enjoying the sport is what it should really be all about and I wasn't much different. I may have been stupid and stubborn to do so – and I've admitted as much earlier – but I basically walked out of Forest and Everton, two very famous and successful clubs, for the simple reason that I wanted to wear that shirt on a Saturday afternoon. I could never have been one of those modern day footballers who sit it out in the reserve team – or not playing altogether – merely to pick up a huge wage packet. Money was never and still isn't as important to me as doing what I really want to do. So I was more than happy to pull on a Kinsley Boys shirt.

I played about four games and took a bit of a hammering – in more ways than one. We were lining up to play Thorne in a Doncaster League game when their number six said to the number five: "You mark the fat kid!" He was referring to David, who was in his usual position of centre forward. Needless to say David helped himself to a hat trick and we won 3-2. Happy days – but that wasn't the last of it. Mistaking the hat trick hero for me, they reported me to the Sheffield and Hallamshire FA saying I was a professional and shouldn't have been playing. I was cleared because I wasn't on anyone's books anymore and hadn't received any compensation for my injuries. But I could have done without the hassle. The worst thing, however, was the tackling – that's a polite way of describing it. Well known players always get a rough time if they finish their careers in the lower divisions or Non League and I was a target. Professionals kick and foul you but do it in a particular way; amateurs are far more reckless and dangerous. But I did what I did for David and I've got no regrets.

That would have been the perfect way to go out but somehow I managed to prolong the agony yet further. My former Forest team mate Martin O'Neill, who was in his very early days as a manager with Grantham Town with John Robertson as his assistant, asked whether I could play a few games for the Non League club. Again, I agreed to help out of loyalty to a friend but was being a fool to myself. I only played twice before I told Martin a combination of the travelling and my knees was just too much. I saw Martin again when he was manager of Leicestershire side Shepshed Charterhouse for a few months where he was allegedly sacked before his managerial career began to take off with Wycombe Wanderers. But could I be so lucky?

9

TC Manager!

NO PRIZES for guessing why this is the shortest chapter – and yet it scores highly among my list of regrets. Perhaps the reason it is so brief is that there is still more to be written and I will have more time in football's hot seat – but, as a betting man, I have to accept that's fairly long odds against.

One of the main talking points of my football career were the managers I played for – the great, the good, the bad and Lawrie McMenemy. Naturally I was bound to pick up a lot from them, even if I did it in my own way. I went on record several times during my playing career that I wanted the opportunity to put all that knowledge and enthusiasm into practice after I finished. Well, I got my chance and, through a mixture of my own mistakes and some bad luck, it was taken away from me all too soon.

My first opportunity to be the boss came through the back door – so to speak – at homely Goole Town in the Northern Premier League. You've probably got the idea by now that I had to be dragged kicking and screaming from the field and, yes, I actually joined the club as a player in 1989. It all happened through a mate called Peter Brown, who is sadly no longer with us. He asked me to come and play for Goole and simply wouldn't go away. I kept on saying no because I knew I was nowhere near fit enough and my last experiences with Kinsley Boys and Grantham Town had given me a fair idea what I'd be letting myself in for. But, finally and probably just to get my mate off my case, I let my heart rule my head and agreed.

I made my debut in a 1-0 defeat in a League Cup tie at

Chorley before making a good start at my new home ground, the Victoria Pleasure Grounds, by scoring twice the following weekend as we began our Northern Premier League campaign with a 3-1 win over Rhyl. By the following Tuesday night I'd become an instant hit with Goole fans by getting the winner at Frickley – but it couldn't last, not on one leg! It was no fun for manager Paddy Buckley either as it developed into a fairly typical Goole season. The club had long been regular strugglers towards the bottom of what is, in all fairness, a tough division. I was in and out of the side as my knee gave me jip and the results continued to go against us. I've honestly got no idea how I played as many games as I did.

With the club by now eight points adrift at the bottom, the inevitable happened with Paddy getting the sack. I hadn't thought too much about what was coming next but when chairman Chris Raywood approached me and asked whether I would become manager it made good sense to give it a go. One thing nobody could argue with was that I represented very good value for money. I ran the club for nothing and even chipped in with cash for the scrambled egg and toast on away trips. I didn't mind at all because I loved every minute.

With a fair degree of irony, one of the first people I did business with was a guy called Ken Richardson, then at Bridlington Town. Ken was the guy who'd already made a stinking name for himself by getting banned from horse racing for life when he substituted a ringer for a dud horse called Flockton Grey. Later he became even better known – and hated – for being the Doncaster Rovers chairman who got jailed for four years after ordering the burning down of the main stand. An even bigger crime in some eyes was that he nearly drove my first league club out of existence. On this occasion, however, it was me who came up trumps as I raided the seasiders to take four players who added quality to our squad – Gary Lockwood, Dave Travis (not the DJ), Gary Lee and Gary Illstone. There was talk of Bridlington getting Paul Showler in return but he ended up at Colne Dynamoes.

We started to get results with the new blood on board and hauled ourselves gradually out of the relegation zone. There were no shortcuts to safety as we faced monster trips to Bangor City and Caenarvon on Tuesday nights – not bad trips for part timers. By the time we went to Caenarvon we knew a draw could well be enough to secure our safety and I surprised a few folk by naming myself in the team. It wasn't so much that I fancied the game but that I didn't have too many bodies to choose from. It wasn't my finest hour and a half on the field as I missed three really good chances to end our agony but it didn't matter a jot as we held out for the 0-0 draw that meant we'd be playing NPL football the following season. The long trip home gave us more time for the post-match party! Celebrating a hard-earned success with genuine lads who'd given their all was for me what being a manager was all about. Bring on next August . . .

Things got hot during the summer as I volunteered for a bit of nostalgia – and went to extra time! The occasion was a match between former Everton and Liverpool players to mark Marine FC manager Roley Howard's 30 years in football. This was the nearest I ever came to playing in a Merseyside derby and I was determined to make the most of it.

I don't remember too much about the actual game although there were some great names on both sides – Howard Kendall and Colin Harvey made brief appearances for Everton alongside Jimmy Gabriel and Terry Darracott whilst David Fairclough, Sammy Lee, David Johnson, Brian Hall and Terry McDermott were all in the Red corner. The real action, however, came off the pitch after we'd all enjoyed a few drinks and a chance to let our hair down – those of us who still had any! The rest of the night will be left to your imagination but, let's just say, I became very friendly with a very lovely lady and tested the bed to its limits to the amusement of Goole secretary Graeme Wilson who still retells the story to anyone who cares to listen.

Having achieved my first mission in management, I began

to piece together my side my first full season in charge. With the help of Peter Brown, who acted as my scout, we brought in some good lads and I used my contacts to get both Forest and Leeds United to send teams to Goole for pre-season friendlies. Both were great nights with Cloughie, in particular, bringing a strong side and several thousand pounds going into club coffers. The chairman spoke with me about the budget for the new season and we both left the meeting well satisfied. He promised me £750 a week to juggle with and I suggested we could keep the budget well inside that figure and use the excess to do something special for the lads at the end of the season by taking them away for a well-earned break.

The first few weeks of the season were magical as we won games and played football I was really proud of. The sight of Goole Town at the top end of the table was unusual and the club was buzzing. I was thoroughly enjoying it for a number of reasons – good passing football was the way I'd always imagined my teams would play and the public were just beginning to vote with their feet by coming into the Victoria Pleasure Grounds in bigger numbers. If only things could have continued like that for a few more months, this chapter could have been a whole lot longer! More relevantly, we could have been looking at promotion to the Alliance, now the Blue Square league, which would have been unheard of territory for Goole. This was all happening on a budget of £450 – a full £300 below the chairman's limit – and, as I still wasn't taking a penny myself, I presumed we were doing well financially. To add to that I'd sold Ian Sansom to Sunderland for £8,000 and after being very impressed by a young striker called Jeremy Smith we'd made another £4,000 by transferring him to Brian Hamilton's Wigan Athletic.

But how wrong I was if I thought this management lark was plain sailing. For then came the bombshell that changed everything. The chairman asked me to see him and I thought he was going to talk about how we could best make the most of our excellent start. Instead he said: "We are going to have to get rid of some players." I couldn't believe my ears.

"Keep this side together and we've got a chance of going up," I replied.

"We can't afford to go up, Terry," he went on.

Now I'm no Carol Vorderman but what this guy was saying didn't add up. Surely we'd bring in more cash by being successful and, as long as we didn't make the common mistake of overstretching ourselves, the future had to be bright.

Then Raywood came to the point: "It's the bonus system I have negotiated with the players. We owe them close to £1,000!"

This was complete news to me. Behind my back, the chairman had negotiated a bonus for each player for every point, so our unexpected success had bitten him in the pocket. Gone was the cash I thought was being kept for an end of season get together, instead the chairman had made a promise he couldn't afford to fulfil. Not only that but guess who was to have the task of explaining the club's mistake to the players? Was I hell! I'd been the one who had talked players into coming to an unfashionable club on low pay – our highest paid lad was Dale Banton, the former York and West Ham striker, on just £60 a week – so I was damned if I was going to tell them we couldn't afford their wages.

When I came down off the roof, I did explain the situation to the lads as best I could and most agreed to give it a couple of weeks to see whether they were going to get paid. The end came at Matlock Town one night when the chairman told me he'd received offers for a couple of our better players and he intended to sell. "You sell them and I'm off," I said. This time there was no room for turning back. That was me finished at Goole Town and what a shame it was for both me and the club.

Had the chairman kept his nose out of it, we could have built a very successful team at Goole and I may have caught the attention of a Football League club looking for an ambitious young manager. It's all pure speculation, of course, but very possible in my opinion. Instead Goole continued to cock up their finances and eventually went out of existence altogether only to re-form again as Goole AFC, thanks to genuine guys such as Graeme Wilson who is still a driving force at the club. As for me, I'm writing about management here rather than doing the job . . .

I did apply for managerial vacancies at both Wednesday and Middlesbrough but didn't get any encouragement from either before I made a mistake which probably cost me very dearly as far as my future prospects were concerned. Because I wanted another job I accepted the post as manager at Mossley, another Northern Premier League club, where I worked with Paul Jones, who I'd played alongside at Huddersfield, as my assistant.

The Lancashire club had been a real force at this level in the late 1970s and early 80s when they won the title twice and were in the top two for five successive seasons. But they had really begun to struggle in recent seasons and, to be fair, I had my card marked by Sammy Mcilroy, the former Manchester United player, who warned me that it would be very difficult. He was right and I went into the lion's den.

My first game was just after Bonfire Night at Trafford in the Manchester Premier Cup where we lost 5-2. Problem was we actually got worse. Barely a month later I was in charge for the very last time; a miserable 6-1 defeat against AFC Emley at our home ground at Seel Park in the Northern Premier League Cup. I was there for just seven games and Paul and I left with a 100 per cent record – seven successive defeats! My defence to that was there was no cash to bring in the right players and the ones I had were never going to be good enough to do the job. Morale was low and too many of the experienced lads decided enough was enough. It was no surprise that at the end of that 1992-93 season Mossley were relegated along with Goole Town.

Non League football has a lot to recommend it with

the closer ties between club officials and players and the supporters and you meet some really genuine football folk at that level. At its best, it reminds you of what football should be all about – the joy of pulling on that shirt and giving your very best on a Saturday afternoon is much the same whether you're at Goole Town playing in front of a few hundred spectators or at Old Trafford entertaining 60,000 to 70,000. But anyone who thinks it's a comfortable shortcut back into the Football League or the Premier League is in for a rude shock. The same financial realities apply in Non League as they do in the fully professional side of the game. It's very easy to end up in a cul-de-sac with a club that has no real prospects of improving and the only way is down. Don't get me wrong, there are people who are rightly recognised as great managers for their achievements in the game. But not even Sir Alex and Jose Mourinho combined could have got Goole Town and Mossley winning every week but I was the one whose reputation took a hammering.

That experience was a real setback but my mate Martin O'Neill advised me to keep on applying, pointing out he'd had plenty of rejections before he really got on the ladder by getting Wycombe Wanderers into the Football League – the rest, of course, being history as he has achieved success at Leicester City, Celtic and Aston Villa and is currently doing so well at Sunderland. Perhaps I should have listened to him and given it another go but sometimes you just get the feeling you've come to the end of the road and need a completely new start. So instead of firing off scatter gun applications and probably ending up with another car crash club like Mossley, I decided enough was enough. I was disillusioned by having the plug pulled out at Goole Town and then my baptism of fire at Mossley. TC was out of here and into a different world altogether.

I have to accept today – 20 years since my sacking at Mossley – my chances of becoming a football manager again are reducing by the day. I've found myself struggling against two or three obstacles – a lot of people have an idea that I'm not the brightest person around which I think is unfair. This perhaps comes from some of the wilful decisions I made in my playing career which I have discussed here as among my biggest regrets. But I am someone who, although not well educated in the traditional sense, thinks very deeply about the game and has been proven right a lot more times than I've been given credit for. Chairmen may also presume I'm confrontational because I've never been shy of expressing my views but I get on with most people. If anything, I'd just describe myself as honest and prefer to get my thoughts out into the open without holding grudges or falling out with folk. Naturally my age and relative lack of managerial experience also now counts against me.

I just find it a bit sad when you read about jobs coming up in the Football League and the same old names appear again and again as candidates – journeymen who have never achieved anything and almost certainly never will, but are still on the ladder and just waiting for someone to forget the past and employ them. Again, if we're going to take football forward in this country and increase the number of English managers, someone, somewhere has got to take a gamble on talent coming through from Non League or people, like me, who are currently not in managerial posts.

I know I raised a few eyebrows a couple of years ago when I applied again for the job at Sheffield Wednesday when Brian Laws was sacked and Alan Irvine was eventually appointed. I offered to do the job – my dream job, of course – for free and many people probably thought it was Terry Curran again going off his head. Here, after all, was a guy who'd been out of football for years suddenly asking for a high profile job. Dave Allen just smiled at me and didn't say a word and I didn't even get a letter acknowledging my interest. But I was serious about it, deadly serious. I love that football club and I'd have gladly worked for them for nothing if I thought I could take them forward. Yes, I know, it would have been a big gamble for them, as it would for me. It's one of the greatest privileges of my life that I was voted as Wednesday's all-time cult hero by the fans in a survey done by *Football Focus* and I still enjoy a really good rapport with people there both when I go to occasional matches at Hillsborough and meet them in everyday life. Losing a few games as their manager would have put some of that popularity at risk, particularly these days when bosses get no respite from instant criticism. But I have real confidence in the way I want to play the game and my ability to motivate people.

If I don't manage again – and I'd only consider a job where there is genuine potential – I will have missed out. After all, having had the chance to learn the good and the bad from the biggest managers in the game in my day, I should have had a head start when it came to management. I did a good job at Goole Town until the chairman mucked things up, then made the mistake of joining a sinking ship at Mossley. Had I bided my time then and got a better offer, perhaps my managerial story would have been altogether different.

10

A Funny Old Business

DID I fall out with football? The answer was 'yes' but then maybe I was never totally in love with it in the first place. Let's put it this way, I was out of the beautiful game for 16 years and didn't miss it too much to be honest – so that must say something

There were many reasons really. For a start, although I'd done more than most to show off on a football field and in a fair few night clubs, I could have done without some of the hassle that comes with the lifestyle. Ok, I could cope with women falling at my feet but being recognised everywhere you go has its drawbacks. It wasn't easy for me to go out for a drink in Sheffield as I'd done the unthinkable and played for both Wednesday and United. When I did, I wanted to be left to myself – or the girl I was trying to pull – rather than be drawn into a conversation about my football career. Don't get me wrong, I've got time for the fans but there's a time and a place. I've also never quite understood why people are so keen on autographs, but we're all different, I suppose.

I was also sick of the arguments. Throughout my career, I'd been raging against authority and there was only going to be one winner – not me! Most of it was my fault but I needed a rest from fighting my corner. For once in my life I enjoyed the idea of being my own boss and not having to depend on anyone else.

I was definitely fed up with the way football was going. Where was the next Willie Johnston, Charlie Cooke, Frank Worthington, Alan Hudson, Johnny Giles or Davie Cooper – super skilled entertainers who had made watching football like going to the finest show? During my career Forest and Everton, where the training was good and the style of play top quality, had been the exceptions rather than the norm. Our coaches were light years behind the continentals and we were being caught up and overtaken by modest football nations. The long ball game ruled supreme and I didn't want anything more to do with it. My 'beautiful game', as I saw it, was becoming more and more difficult to find.

Going into the pallets business full time was my obvious next move. So I decided to kick football into touch and join up full time with my mate Gary Oakley. I'd been putting my spare time hours into it for several years, so it wasn't too much of a culture change to team up with Gary at Knottingley Petrol Station. Football never got a second thought, although it opened a few doors for me business-wise as people recognised me and liked to talk about the game. We did very well, too, continuing to make about £2,000 a week each for three good years before being dealt a blow. We were then forced to move and seek new premises as owners Texaco said they were selling the petrol station to make way for some industrial units. This resulted in the two of us going our separate ways as it didn't prove possible to find a replacement site to accommodate both – so Gary moved to the Ferrybridge Services and I bought 3.5 acres of land at Micklefield where I also rented the Woodlands transport cafe.

There I worked either on my own or with one other lad and really enjoyed myself. The cafe was a good business in itself, particularly as lorry drivers also enjoyed coming to talk to a former footballer but, once again, the pallets brought in the majority of the cash. Everyone was undercutting everyone else at that time, so I bought and sold pallets back into the trade at a profit. I wasn't short of volume with 21 stacks packed 60 high. Typically, I'd buy ten pallets from a wagon – eight would be fine, whilst the other two might need some work or be useful for stripping down. I was working long hours – like most who run their own business – but it was never more than five days a week, so there was still time for socialising.

I brought in my own ideas to improve a cafe that had always been a popular stopping-off point. My thinking was to up the quality and bank on customers showing their appreciation by coming back for more. So in came the best back bacon, Nescafe and 'bottomless' tea with the freezer constantly restocked. Not everyone agreed with most complaints being about the tea going up in price from 45p to 70p even though they were getting a far bigger cuppa. But results were good with us doing food all the way through the day until 10pm and the bar often open until 3am. I was on my way in business and having a good time.

Running my own show was all the more fun as I was now single. I was working hard but there was always more than enough time both on the job and off it to weave my magic with the ladies. In fact it couldn't have been more perfect as I had my own eating place and bar to entertain anyone I fancied. My living accommodation – a bungalow – was ideal being bang next to the transport cafe and, thanks to my childhood training, I had no problems living on my own. This added up to the chance to have my cake and eat it. Soon I had about four women on the go – three married – and none any the wiser about the existence of the others. Who needed football and all that endless hassle?

Going out with more than one woman does cause the odd problem such as who do you invite to the Christmas party? I thought of a good answer – all four! We were having a do at the transport cafe a week before Christmas 1994 so, not wanting to disappoint anyone, I invited the lot! How the hell was I going to get away with it? Well, my thinking was this: as I was the host for the night, I'd spend some time with each, then say I needed to be sociable and mingle as it was my party. Then I'd move onto the next girlfriend! It also helped that the three married women all had to be back home at certain times.

They all turned up and my plan didn't quite work although not for the reason you are probably thinking. For in through the door came woman number five! You couldn't make this up, could you? Unknown to me, a woman called Lynne, who lived in the village, was getting ready to go to the party. Apparently she had friends working with me and had been well warned about the randy former footballer owner she needed to steer well clear of!

I was none the wiser, of course, and my eyes spied a very tasty looking brunette sipping a drink. Even though I wasn't short of female company, I was intrigued – enough to send her a message that she was welcome to come to the bar and share a drink. The message back was on the lines of 'well, if he wants to do so, he better come and ask himself!' That wasn't a 'no' and certainly gave me room for another approach. So when she came to the bar to order another drink, I made my move. I asked her what she was drinking and she said "a Tia Maria". "You what! This is a transport cafe – not a five-star hotel," I replied. So she settled for a Bacardi and Coke instead and we got chatting . . . and chatting and chatting! Suddenly the other women in the room didn't matter; I was really enjoying myself with this attractive stranger.

We were obviously hitting it off big time because the conversation turned to heavier subjects. I found out that she, like me, was divorced and was also a mother of one. She asked me whether I had any experience of children and I made her laugh by saying I enjoyed taking my nieces everywhere I went. "How old are they?" she asked expectantly. "They're 27 and 28," I replied. "I'm 28 too," she said. "Good, I can take you everywhere with me too!" I added cheekily. She asked whether it would make any difference that she had an 18-month-old son. Blimey, she must really like me. The answer was it didn't and I had nothing against the little things – I even used to be one myself. Perhaps I still was!

Anyway, the evening came to an end at about 3am and I did the gentlemanly thing by not pressing things too far but ensuring we exchanged telephone numbers. I asked her when would be a good night to take her out and she said that a few days later, December 20, was her 29th birthday.

I didn't want to wait that long. I phoned her to ask if she'd like to come over for a coffee and suggested she brought her son Tom with her as I could introduce him to my leather football. We continued meeting up and had a really good night out at an Italian restaurant on her birthday. This time she really could have a Tia Maria. Luck was with me during this early stage of our courtship as I managed to ensure none of the other women called on me at the wrong time during the next couple of weeks until I was able to tell them straight that I was now with someone.

Lynne had a problem after the excitement of Christmas and New Year died down – she had to go into hospital for an operation. I took her son Tom to see her but then came the next obstacle: Lynne wasn't supposed to do any physical work for a while and the hospital weren't keen on her going home as she'd have to look after herself and her son. So I told her she was welcome to stay at mine and that was that – 17 years later she's definitely back on her feet and she's still with me! At long last – and in the most unexpected of circumstances – I found a woman who could tame me. It happens to most of us eventually, you know.

As my private life took a step forward, so did my business life. In 1996 I approached the owners of the site, a Mr and Mrs Braithwaite, and bought it from them for £540,000. I had been taking about £7,000 a week from the cafe alone and reckoned a mortgage of £5,000 a month to pay it off within nine years would be a good investment. I should have been right – the deal could so easily have seen me set up for life but I'd missed something very important and paid a very heavy price for it.

The nightmare started when, after three more successful and enjoyable years, I got a phone call from the local highways department informing me about a new link road from the M1. Worst of all this was going to mean one side of the road leading to my property being shut off to traffic. My business would be devastated at a stroke. I couldn't believe it. Takings were soon down to an all-time low of £75 per day, the pallet business was also suffering from the access problems and my headaches were mounting. With a wage bill of £2,000 a week, plus the mortgage and hefty bills for electricity, gas and water to pay for, I was suddenly heading for potential financial ruin.

I'd put my heart and soul into this place, not sparing the cash in trying to improve it. Altogether I'd spent £200,000 turning a transport café into a motel with 12 rooms, including several doubles, and tiled it from top to bottom. I was in no mood to give up at the first obstacle, so gave it one more shot. I closed down the transport café and reopened as an Italian restaurant called Balodovinos with a reduced but well paid staff. Lynne worked at the front of house and we had a very good first couple of months, quite frequently filling all 100 covers.

From having folk come into the transport cafe and spending 70p on a cuppa, we were hosting couples in the restaurant spending £25 to £30 a head. But then came a bolt out of the blue that caused me to change direction once again. I got an offer from Langtree Homes of £1.25m for the site. Part of the attraction for them was that my site provided access to 38 acres of potential prime building land, so they were prepared also to pay me £2.95m for the right of way should they decide to build on it within the next 20 years. That rider gave their offer an even bigger edge over their housing development rivals Barretts who offered a straight £1m. It was a no-brainer for me – I just had to accept, take the money and run. However much I had enjoyed running my own business, including the Italian restaurant, this was a way out of a financial hole and security for the future thrown in as well. The timing was fantastic. Lynne was pregnant with our son, Jock, so this would be the ultimate new start both for me and my new family with our financial future totally sorted. Too good to be true? You've got it . . .

My biggest mistake was trusting a family solicitor. I should have gone to a specialist land solicitor but the bloke said he could handle the job and I believed him. You'll not have heard me say this too often in this book but I should have also listened to my partner Lynne. For when it came to signing the contracts, she was far from happy.

The figure of £1.25m was there in black and white but the deal seemed open-ended. There wasn't any indication whether this was a gross or net amount. Lynne put it directly to the solicitor that they could still legally come up with a reduced final payment. She argued that the way the contract was worded they could knock the bid down and offer us £1 for the site if they wanted to. He agreed it was possible but, in practice, there was no way they'd do so. I was swayed by the fact they were giving us a £32,000 deposit which would get me out of my immediate cash crisis. So I signed the contract and closed down the restaurant as soon as the money hit my account having been told everything would be finalised within six months

You've probably guessed the rest by now. A man from Langtree Homes came bearing a document with a final payment figure of just £311,000. They had knocked off substantial amounts for a variety of issues including £35,000 for contamination of fuel, £75,000 for the demolition of buildings, a cool £450,000 to provide the council with an acre of land for green space, £40,000 consultancy fees, plus other odds and sods. Lynne may have seen what was coming but we were stunned. There was no way I could accept having the goalposts moved so far. We were by now very angry with our solicitor. If Lynne, a lay person, had spotted the loophole that Langtrees had ruthlessly exploited, how come he hadn't? It was a question that occupied our minds for months, even years.

Next step on what was becoming a very muddy path was to hire another solicitor and try to sue our original one. Eventually we went to a tribunal in London at which the offer was set at £395,000 but our new solicitor advised us against accepting, advising that we could get more if we went to court. But then when we got to the next stage he warned that, although he expected us to win, we could very well end up paying substantial costs, including his and our solicitor's, should we lose. This could have led me down the road to bankruptcy. Finally, an even further reduced figure of £186,000 was put on the table which I felt I had little choice but to accept. So instead of making a good profit from the land, I'd been forced to settle for a figure that was less than what I still owed on the mortgage.

Legal action had dragged on and on and was only finally done and dusted in 2004. By now, you know I'm a laid back character who is not obsessed with money but I've got to admit I was furious with the outcome. If it hadn't been for the fact I was responsible for two children, I may well have resorted to violence to sort it out. Honestly. Worst of all was the deal should have enabled me to give my children financial security but that was taken away from me. Personally, thanks to my football pension – yet another thing I'm grateful to Cloughie for – I was ok but this was beyond a joke. You can imagine how much stress it caused in our relationship, too, as Lynne was, quite rightly, angry with me for being so naive.

That kind of crisis, however, leads you one of two ways. Either you remain bitter all your life and perhaps go down a self destructive road of drinking or worse or you make a decision to move on. The latter is what I did. I don't spent every waking second thinking about it now, even though we live only a few miles away from the site. I know that should Langtree Homes build on their land within the next eight years, there could still be a happy outcome for us as they would then owe me my £2.95m.

But I couldn't afford to sit on my backside and wait for that. So I went back to what I knew best and went into football coaching, mostly for the sake of my young son.

11

Older, Wiser and Still Thinking of England

YOU know what I'd like as a birthday present? A new pair of legs! Not necessarily to play football, but I'd love to be able to run around in training and generally enjoy myself with my family without being constantly reminded of the cost of playing the sport I loved.

Time really does change everything – well, almost everything. The Terry Curran you met earlier in this book was a tearaway striker, a motor mouth with a habit of talking himself into trouble, a womaniser and a lad with a dream of playing football for England. Today, I still talk as fast – with a bit more sense than I managed back then – but everything else is a lot slower! I'm a semi-cripple, barely able to walk let alone run or play football, but a proud parent and family man at last – and I still have a dream for the future of football in this country.

I suppose you can call me a willing victim of the cortisone generation. Fans would have a real shock if they lined up a team of football stars of my age. They'd discover a group of arthritis suffering geriatrics who have paid a long-term price for 15 minutes of fame. I can trace my knackered knees back to that horrific injury at Forest. The 'sports scientists' of my day told me I'd have an operation and be as good as new. Instead I'll carry the effects of that accidental tackle for life. The cortisone injections I had – the first at Saints, three more at Wednesday and the last at Everton – merely masked the pain to warn me something was wrong. The knee just felt numb for a couple of days whilst the jab took its effect, then came the bliss of six months without pain. We all know now that's not the end of the story.

We also played a lot more while we were injured. If anyone had mentioned the phrase 'squad rotation' in my day no one would have had a clue what you were talking about. It would have been difficult in any case to rotate the same 15 or 16 players and come up with different teams. The way I saw it was this: basically if I could walk, I'd declare myself fit. Many others were the same.

My body probably took extra toll because of the type of player I was – always being eager to take on the full back or central defender and try them out for pace made me an obvious target for those steel studs. And, boy, did they hurt when I was on the receiving end. I hate to think how many managers told defenders to 'kick Curran and see whether he'll take you on then!' I didn't help my own cause because, whatever Peter Taylor thought, I was a brave lad who responded to heavy treatment by fighting fire with fire.

In today's compensation culture, I could probably have claimed a few bob from my clubs or opponents for the knocks I took but, to me, it was all part of the game I loved to play. I took the rough with the smooth and that's why I'm shuffling about like a man a good deal older. Good job John Haselden doesn't see me now or he'd take pity on me! Of course, it's frustrating when I've been a fit bloke that I can't join in football training or enjoy a game of tennis but I enjoy the vast majority of my life and always will. My cup has always been half full rather than half empty and I regard myself as luckier than a lot of folk in this world.

I had a further shock in the summer of 2011, however. For ages and ages I'd been putting off surgery on my knees – the PFA were going to help me with a replacement knee joint at one stage – and I went to see a specialist in Sheffield, expecting that, at long last, a date would be set.

"Your knees aren't good," he told me. "But I'm more

worried about your ankle. It's collapsed completely and you're going to need an operation straightaway." I was given two choices: either a false ankle joint which would last five years before I'd have to go under the knife all over again or it could be fused and pinned, a more complicated procedure with a longer recovery time.

I bit the bullet and chose the second option as it should now last a lifetime. I was in and out of the Claremont Hospital in just a couple of days but the next three months were no joke. I had to keep my leg raised for six weeks and sleeping downstairs on the sofa bed was the very least of my problems. The summer was so painful it was almost as bad as watching England in the World Cup the year before. Finally in January 2012 I got the all-clear from the specialist – until they call me in again to fix my knees, of course.

My hectic lifestyle with women has been replaced by as close as I'll ever get to routine. I've now been with my partner Lynne for 17 years and I'm a parent both to Tom and to Jock, who is 11 years old. Lynne is now a teacher and doing very well. After all, if she can put me in my place, she must be pretty good. Being a father is one of the best and hardest things in life. If you are a parent, you will probably know what I mean by that. Nothing in the world gives you more pride than seeing your boy or girl grow up and develop – yet, at the same time, you know they are going to make mistakes and there's nothing you can do to prevent some of them happening. I regard myself as very lucky that all this has happened to me after so long when I didn't have any family responsibilities. I can honestly say that, if I had my life all over again, and it was a choice of being either a footballer or a parent – I'd choose being a parent. I can't say how I feel any more clearly than that.

Becoming a Dad was very strongly linked with my return to football and my work as a coach. I didn't go back because I couldn't live without the game – I've proved that to be wrong – but mostly to encourage Jock as a footballer. The last thing

I'd ever want to do is put pressure on the lad because I know he is entering a football world very different to the one in which I launched my career. I'd say the same thing to my son as I would to any talented youngster: you can have all the ability in the world but there's no telling at that age whether you're going to make it as a professional. What he and others need to do is work hard at both their game and at school. I got a lot of my education from intelligent folk as I made my way in adult life because I didn't give school enough time and attention. I got away with it to a certain extent but today's youngsters can't afford to think the same way. There is nothing so important to a young person as education.

Currently I'm working with Jock's age group at Doncaster Rovers' Centre of Excellence at the Keepmoat Stadium. As I've said before, it's brilliant to be at Donny, my first professional club and one that has progressed so much in recent years. If someone had told me when I left Belle Vue that 30 odd years later the club would be at a new ground and spent good years in the second level of English football, I'd have thought they were dafter than me! It's my second spell with the club as I've also worked in similar roles at both Barnsley and Rotherham United and it's a job I genuinely love doing. Being the type of person I am, it's not a case of just doing the training sessions and overseeing our games against clubs on a Sunday. The job plays a big part in the rest of my week as well. I enjoy chatting to parents about the development of their boys and I'm always thinking about what I'm doing. It's a big responsibility to be working with young people dreaming like I did of a career in football and I've already learned so much.

Yes, a lot of things I have seen frustrate me greatly. For, although football in this country owes Howard Wilkinson a debt for founding the academy system, we have taken a very good idea and built on it very badly. Nobody disagrees with the idea that if we want to overhaul football in England and get back to the stage when the national team is on top of the world it has to start with the youngsters. The problem is how we pick those youngsters, how we coach them and what we are really trying to achieve. We haven't had nearly 50 years of failure at international level, a failing highlighted yet again at Euro 2012, because of bad luck. The reasons go far beyond the academy system, of course, but they do include the way we have developed the best young talent in this country over the past two decades.

It was a massive own goal for our future that people such as Wilkinson and Charlie Hughes, who also had such influence at the FA, were such big fans of the long ball game. Hughes was the guy you may remember who came up with all sorts of statistics to show that the best way to score goals was to hoof the ball into the penalty area as quickly as possible. Then we had the shambles of Graham Taylor, who'd done so well taking Watford from the Fourth Division to the First, promoting his version of kick and rush at international level. Can you see the irony of what I'm saying here? I was always fighting a losing battle with the likes of Big Jack, Lawrie McMenemy and others when I told them their training methods and tactics were outdated. That was in the late 1970s and 1980s! Here we are in 2012 and we are still making some of the same basic mistakes.

First thing we have to get right is that we're in the business of producing footballers not athletes. For too long we've rejected talented lads because they are small for their age or haven't filled out as quickly as expected and encouraged those who look as if they have the right build to get up and down the pitch. That's madness. Do you play football with a pole vault or a hammer or on a race track? No, we don't – we play it with a ball. Let's take a look at the Barcelona super model, that should be the blueprint for our football in the future. Some of the great players in their first team that is dominating Europe and providing most of Spain's national side are not fantastic athletes. But they are brilliant technically. Why are they so brilliant? Yes, they had to have natural ability to start with, but they have been coached the right way from day one.

As Cloughie constantly said, the football is their friend, so they ensure it stays with their mates. If you get a lad who is physically behind the others but does have ability, just drop them down a year and give nature the chance to take its course.

Another major problem lies with our coaches. I was shocked doing my UEFA 'B' badge that we were supposed to give instruction on how to hit 20 and 30-yard balls. Proof we're still struggling to get away from the dark ages of long ball football. People in this country used to drool when David Beckham hit a 45-yard pass from one end of the pitch to the other that found its target – or narrowly failed. Instead at Barcelona they applaud the five-yard pass that always finds a team mate and opens up room for the move to progress. Just listen to the parents when their youngsters are playing: "hump it", "get rid of it", "clear it" they shout. We are still obsessed with the long ball game – get it into opposition territory and fight for the second ball and knockdowns. That may still get results in the 100mph all-action Premier League but isn't nearly as successful in Europe, despite Chelsea's success in 2012, or at international level where the game is far more technical. Manchester United and Manchester City's group stage exits in the Champions League in 2011-12 were good indications of the decline. Chelsea may have defied them through sheer defensive grit and good luck but generally we are not on the same planet as Barcelona.

One step forward is the introduction of an elite system at academy level. This will, in the short term, make my job harder at a club like Doncaster Rovers but will eventually bring benefits to all. The old system encouraged youngsters to stay at lower clubs because of the high fees required for the top sides to sign them. But now there will be a ceiling of £135,000 which will mean more of the cream of the crop will get their football education at United, City, Chelsea and Arsenal and others. Other sports have been ahead of football for years in their introduction of elite squads and academies, usually taking all the best players and putting them together. These involve taking youngsters out of school and their clubs and enabling them to train, learn and live together, often alongside elite youngsters from other sports. Naturally we can't remove footballers from club life or centrally contract them in the way England have done with their cricket team and shot to the top of the world after so long. But we can, and now will, put the best young talent with the best coaches and the best facilities at the top clubs. Before this, too much coaching time was wasted on dealing with the less talented youngsters whilst the others kicked their heels.

In the same way, there's nothing to be gained from Manchester United lads beating Barnsley 16-1 in an academy game – and I'm not intending to have a go at the Tykes there. It neither benefits the winning team because they are not being stretched nor the young players on the receiving end. The elite players should be playing their matches against other elite youngsters

The new system will also be good for the youngsters and their education. Some no doubt will struggle with their studies and if left in schools will show about as much enthusiasm as I did. But I think they will do better when put together with their football mates who face the same challenge. Also when the youngsters get to under 18 level only a proportion will be signed by the top clubs and therefore you will have a good number going back to the likes of Doncaster, Barnsley and Rotherham, having had a far better football education than if they'd stayed there for years. Hopefully, this can lead to an increase in standards all round.

We are also suffering nationally because of the very influx of continental players and managers that I forecast all those years ago and has undoubtedly improved our game in many ways. I've got nothing at all against established players from any country coming into the Premier or Football League but I do think it has been overdone at academy level. It's been too easy for too long for clubs to bring in youngsters from Europe, where they have already received their football grounding, meaning fewer opportunities for lads from this country.

We have helped to create a situation in which the national team has been pushed to the very back of a long list of priorities. Take the current Premier League as an example. If you take the bosses of the top clubs such as Sir Alex Ferguson, Roberto Mancini and Arsene Wenger, do you really think the England team features in their thinking? Sir Alex, for all his qualities and what he has achieved for a club very close to my heart, has always made it as difficult as possible for England to have full use of his players. He was reportedly threatening to sue England in 2006 if Wayne Rooney, who was fighting to return to the World Cup after being injured at United, was injured again. Yet he never had any problem releasing Darren Fletcher to play for Scotland before the midfielder's current illness. The reason of course is that Sir Alex is Scottish and he will naturally support his country's cause as far as possible.

It's the same with Wenger, whom I regard as one of the best managers in world football. He'd do anything to discourage Theo Walcott from playing for England Under 21s but his French lads always join up with their country. If you want to check out what I'm saying, take a look the next time there's a major tournament at Under 21 level or below and see how few of our Premier League players take part compared with the top stars from Spain, Holland and Germany who gain vital experience of tournament football. It's little surprise they all have a far better record than us in both the World Cup and European Championships because their players have got used to the demands of spending weeks in a training camp and producing their very best form over a number of high pressure games played in fairly quick succession.

I would like to see more English managers in the Premier League and also a policy of English managers for the national team from this point on with Roy Hodgson being the rule rather than the exception. I'm not being anti-foreign in any way I just happen to believe that England should have an English manager, a Scot should manage Scotland and a German should manage Germany. There's no reason even for the smaller countries seeking to make their way in world football not to choose their own coaches with perhaps someone from a world power alongside them.

I don't think that either Sven-Goran Eriksson or Fabio Capello, for all their vast experience, added very much to our team as they sandwiched a terrible English choice in Steve McClaren. They've fallen time after time into the same old trap of sticking with players fast disappearing over the hill because they don't trust younger alternatives and trying to fit stars into a team. The Frank Lampard and Steven Gerrard situation has been a prime example. When you've got one of the most talented central midfielders we've produced for generations in Gerrard and too often play him wide because you've got to accommodate Lampard, you're missing the point in how to build a team. Countries such as Spain and Holland don't make the same mistake. They pick a balanced side with no one getting his name on the teamsheet just because they're too big to leave out.

I have to concede that Hodgson's appointment surprised me as I couldn't see past Harry Redknapp being offered the England job. He fits the bill in many respects – he is English, has a good record and his teams enjoy playing for him and always produce good football. It tells you a lot, however, about the problems we currently have that there didn't appear to be many out there to challenge him. Redknapp's teams do generally play the right way as we've got to get rid of the long ball if we are ever going to challenge the best teams in world football. Instead what I saw in 2010 and again in Euro 2012 was a team that often looked uneasy in possession. All the good teams do is then drop off to encourage us to go long and give us a chasing when they win it back. So many England performances tail off in the last 20 minutes as it becomes impossible to harry opponents for 90 minutes, particularly in the hot conditions in recent finals.

I watch a hell of a lot of current day football – seeing most of Donny's home matches at the Keepmoat Stadium, Wednesday when I can make it to Hillsborough and some of the world's best players courtesy of television. I'm not one of those old timers who knock the modern game for the sake of it. The game's improved in many ways – just as in other areas of life – and yet still has its challenges. The curse of the long ball remains a feature of our game and is one of the main reasons that I and so many other English football fans still hark back to 1966.

I was just one of thousands of impressionable youngsters inspired by that great day to take up the game and keep England at the top of the football world. Unfortunately I fell short of my goal of playing for my country and my country has consistently failed to produce at the top level. I will, of course, continue to dream on with my passions – I still believe Sheffield Wednesday's place is in the Premier League and I look forward to being at a full Hillsborough to welcome the best teams in our land. But I can't see England winning another major tournament in my lifetime unless there is a major change in the way we coach our young players of the future.

Hopefully young footballers reading this will learn something from my mistakes. You probably wondered when you first picked up my story why I called it *Regrets*. After all, I was supposed to be the rebel who played the game as if tomorrow didn't exist. The truth was, as my friend Reidy so rightly says, that I under achieved. I can't help but wonder what would have happened had I not suffered that terrible injury at Forest and if I'd stayed injury-free when I had my last big chance in the game at Everton. But mostly I got it wrong myself. I picked too many arguments, ruffled too many feathers and took too many wrong turnings.

You can ignore everything else in this book, if you wish, but remember this advice that I give to my youngsters at Doncaster Rovers: football is a passionate game, but the difference between succeeding and failing isn't really a matter of how hard you strive – it's all about decision making. The player who has that extra split second to see what is going on around him, weigh up the options and choose the right one is the one I would want in my team. So keep a cool head, make the right decisions and remember that your football career won't last forever.

I'm not a bitter man – never have been, never will be. To have played as many games as I did, get to Wembley, be part of a couple of promotion campaigns and claim a First Division winners' medal was fantastic. To be remembered so fondly by fans of Sheffield Wednesday, the club I still love, is unbelievable. I lived to excess off-the-field and left everyone with more than my fair share of special and, let's face it, unusual moments on it.

Now, hopefully, as a Dad, a coach and now author, I'm passing on my experience both good and bad. Enjoy life, enjoy your football – and make sure you have no regrets!

Appendix: My Dream Team

EVERYONE has their idea of a dream team. Mine isn't the best 11 players that ever lived – that's why you don't see the likes of Messi, Best and Maradona in this line up – but the best I played with. Let's face it, I had plenty to choose from considering I had 13 English clubs and no doubt it'll surprise a few that there are three Derby County players in it from a team that finished mid-table and just two of my former Nottingham Forest colleagues who went on to win a European Cup double. But I've made my selection on what I saw and, as you know by now, I'm nothing but honest. Best represented – not surprisingly – are Everton with four. Let's face it, that side was by far the best that I had the pleasure of playing for. Apologies to Sheffield Wednesday fans, by the way, for not having any Owls in the team but that would have been stretching my loyalty a little too far. If you like, you can sit me on the bench – never my favourite position, but I'd happily have done it just to see this team play!

Goalkeeper – Neville Southall (Everton): I never played in the same team as Peter Shilton at Forest but, even if I had, I would still have picked Neville Southall. He ruled in an era when Britain seemed to have all the best goalkeepers – Shilts, Ray Clemence and Pat Jennings being chief among them. Today when young Joe Hart at Manchester City is out there on his own, you'd have appreciated Neville even more. Every team looks to have confidence in its last line of defence and Neville oozed it. It didn't matter whether the ball was in the air or on the floor, you never expected the guy to be beaten.

Many goalkeepers lived in fear of big men coming into their penalty area, this man just bullied them. He'd win the ball and almost knock his opponent's block off. The difference he made when he took over from Jim Arnold, not a bad keeper himself, was remarkable. Great teams need great goalies and there wasn't a better one in Europe, if not the world.

Right back – Viv Anderson (Nottingham Forest): Again it was a choice between one of Cloughie's brightest stars and a Merseysider and this time the former gets the nod for me. I rated 'Spider' very highly. He was the best defender in a side that went on to concede goals at a miserly rate after I left and was a real force going forward with those long legs that used to nick the ball away from players just when you thought he'd been beaten. He was also a pioneer in being the first black player to win a full international cap for England, stuffing all that horrible abuse he suffered down people's throats. Spider had to be top rate to nick this position ahead of Gary Stevens, his rival for the England spot and a truly class act.

Centre back – Roy McFarland (Derby County): Let's face it, there was no shortage of candidates for this position – Kevin Ratcliffe was a fantastic defender for Everton and, in a very different way to McFarland, Larry Lloyd became part of one of the best defences of its time at Forest. But, if you were looking for pure quality, there's no way you could look past Roy Mc. In my team, I want to have defenders happy in possession rather than Row Z merchants and Roy was very much ahead of his time as a centre back with composure and class. It's not surprising at all that he won two league titles – one under Cloughie, the other with Dave Mackay – but I find it strange he only won 28 England caps. It should have been many more.

Centre back – Colin Todd (Derby County): I like the idea of selecting a real-life partnership in my back four and Todd formed one of the best defensive barriers with Roy McFarland. But, let's face it, there was no problem selecting Toddy on his own merit. If there's been an England defender more like Bobby Moore in his calm and composed manner on the ball, I haven't seen him. When you think about great players in any sport, they always seem to have that extra split second whether it be a test match batsman, a top tennis player or a footballer. Again, something was very wrong for Toddy to only get 27 international caps.

Left back – David Nish (Derby County): Must have been a midfield player at some stage in his life to be that good on the ball. The Rams paid a record transfer fee of £225,000 to bring him across the East Midlands from Leicester City and he paid them back many times over. We've been crying out for defenders with the confidence to keep and use the ball before and since but Nishie was the one who stood out for being able to do just that. That would have been no good but for the fact he also did his main job so well as a defender.

Centre midfield – Alan Ball (Southampton): I know he was a great mate of mine but Bally was world class. Often people talk about the players of yesterday and query whether they could have made it in the much faster game of today, but you wouldn't have to ask that question of Bally. His one and two-touch passing was years ahead of its time and he'd have stood out in any of England's midfield line ups since. Obviously, he was coming towards the end of his great career when I played with him but that only left me with the thought that I'd have loved to have seen him in his prime. The ultimate compliment is that he's the one star from the past who'd have slotted into Barcelona's midfield as if he was born for the job. Now I can't say better than that.

Centre midfield – Peter Reid (Everton): Every team needs a midfield dynamo, someone who breaks up opposition play and sets your team in motion and Reidy was the best I ever saw at doing just that. At his best, which he was at Goodison Park, he must have been a complete nightmare to play against. I don't think Everton would have gone on to win half the trophies we did if Howard Kendall had sold him to Burnley as he was thinking of doing. There was just one thing that separated a top class player from a truly great one – had Reidy had just that extra half yard of pace, he'd have got himself on the scoresheet more often and would never have been off England's teamsheet.

Right wing – John Robertson (Nottingham Forest): I watched him do it thousands of times and I still don't know how he managed it. The 'fat' guy was almost Houdini-like in the way he'd battle his way out of a tight corner. There were usually two defenders on him during Forest's glory days but he'd sway one way, nick the ball past them and then deliver the best cross you'll ever see. Robbo never looked a player off the pitch, but on it he was Cloughie's best by a mile – and he knew it. Makes me proud to think I was the senior winger at the City Ground for a while but sad that I didn't stay to see him weave his magic in the First Division and the European Cup in which he made and scored Forest's winning goals in 1979 and 1980. I know you're going to say he was a left rather than a right winger, but his right was his best foot and I'd have played him knowing exactly what he'd give my team.

Centre forward – Andy Gray (Everton): Never known a braver player in my life. His knees were more knackered than mine when he was at Goodison Park but if you ever wanted a forward to throw himself at the ball in a crowded penalty area it was Andy. Perhaps he'd been at his very best at Aston Villa, but it was at Everton where he landed most of his trophies including crucial goals in the semi final and final of the European Cup Winners Cup and where he battered poor Watford goalkeeper Steve Sherwood at Wembley.

Centre forward – Charlie George (Derby County): Biggest compliment I can pay this guy is that I link him in my mind to George Best. He really was that talented. Had already been a legend at Arsenal when he came to Derby and was a major part in their success. I never really found top gear at the Baseball Ground but watching this guy play almost made up for it. If we're ever going to win international competitions again, we need to unearth another player like him and ensure he wins 90 to 100 caps. The fact he played only once showed how far our England managers were behind the times.

Left wing – Kevin Sheedy (Everton): Had a left foot to die for, in fact it was more like a wand to be honest. There were some fantastic players in my Everton team which won the First Division title and the European Cup Winners' Cup and Sheedy was right up there with the best of them. When you've got a natural left footer in your side, it gives you great balance and that's what I'd want in my team. Apart from his general play, the Republic of Ireland international was a winger who actually scored goals. They tell me that in the 1980s nobody scored more goals from free kicks than Kevin and I can well believe it. One day he curled a 25-yarder into the top corner but had to re-take it because of an infringement – so he stepped up and did exactly the same thing but in the opposite corner. Can't say any better than that.